How to Stop Paying Your Mortgage Without Leaving Home

By William Orion and Jana J. Perlman

2012 Edition

How to Stop Paying Your Mortgage Without Leaving Home
New 2012 edition!

Retake the sovereignty that's **already yours!**

Stay in your own house while legally exempting yourself from invalid mortgage paper.

- Banish banksters
- Reclaim rights
- Convince courts
- Frustrate foreclosers

By William Orion and Jana J. Perlman

When did the dream house turn into a debtors' prison?

When did "buying land" start to mean "going underwater?"

Is it really legal and moral to "get out of your mortgage free?"

This e-book reveals the dirty little secrets of the real estate industry. This is not your grandfather's guide to realty transactions: it's a potent tool to slay the zombie monsters created by big-government regulation, big-bank manipulation, and above all the big complacent ignorance that keeps people in chains.

Find out the common name of the undead medieval beast that has entombed millions of Americans!

Find out how to make your home your own castle once again!

Read "Homestead Security" today and learn how people like you are already exerting their nonpayment rights from the comfort of their own homes!

All incidents described herein are real summaries of actual victories by actual homebuyers who conquered the thirty-year mortgage. In some cases, names were changed to protect the privacy of the successful individuals, but their successes are no less sweet. All reasonable attempts have been made to describe applicable laws and other content accurately, but this book of success stories is not written by lawyers and does not constitute legal advice or advice of any kind. These testimonies are provided for information only and no guarantee or representation is made whatsoever, whether of freedom from inaccuracies or omissions, of the fitness of this information for any purpose, or of any other fact or statement. Your mileage may vary. It is your responsibility to consult a lawyer, accountant, and/or real estate agent licensed by the appropriate agency of your state before making any decisions that require professional services. By continuing to read this information you take and accept full and complete responsibility for all your actions, whether related to the information or not.

Copyright (C) 2012 Will Orion and Jana J. Perlman.
All rights reserved under state and federal law and the law of nations.
Copyright number 1-809641812.

Introduction

When did the dream house turn into a debtors' prison? When did "buying land" start to mean, "going underwater?"

Once upon a time in America, keeping up with the Joneses used to mean every family could own their own home free and clear. As time went on, people started buying younger and younger, they invested less and less up front, they wanted more and more built-in conveniences, and they extended their mortgages longer and longer. Before the next generation could realize it, they had become lifetime slaves in homes that were their own and yet not their own.

That's the thirty- and forty-year mortgage; a lifetime career of indentured servitude. Nowadays the Joneses are hardly recognizable because the neighborhood changes so often. Today our neighbors are "flipping" mansions, risking fixer-ups, or even house-hopping. When you hear they are sending jingle mail (mailing the house keys back to the bank) you know they're gone for good, gone on to the next big speculation.

Meanwhile, back at the ranch, you've locked yourself into a fixed rate, an adjustable rate, a refi rate, -some- rate of interest that keeps biting back every time you make that monthly mortgage payment. The more years you still have ahead, the bigger the bite. Most folks are paying more interest than principal: and that means they're slaves. Slaves in their own homes. The will-o'-the-wisp of debt-free homeownership seems just as imaginary as the land grabs that those itinerant neighbors are investing all their guesswork in.

Usually, you note, those who play real estate like a game end up losing or amassing fortunes. Just like in Monopoly, the game that is designed to make everybody go bankrupt, with two exceptions; the banker and the player that somehow finagled every other player's real estate and money away from them. Some call it luck, but how "lucky" is it when the same Monopoly player wins most every time?

No, you mutter from within your prison, much wiser and safer and more scrupulous to put one's nose to the daily grindstone and cough up the mortgage payment regularly for the next twenty-eight years. Once or twice you hear about an exception, the great deals the Joneses and the Smiths worked out on their homes. They figured out how to play the game; and won! Then suddenly, the bankers closed the doors while you have a rope around your neck looking for a break.

These days, you probably haven't heard of any good deals lately. You start to wonder when the next great deal will come along in your neighborhood. But here's the good news: you can make it happen. You yourself. In this book you can find all the tools you need to make the next great real estate deal in your neighborhood happen right in your own home!

If your home has become a debtors' prison that keeps you at the mercy of the banksters who dictated your loan, I'll bet they never told you that - you hold the key! In America, no mortgage overlord has any authority whatsoever to steal the key to your own home. I'm not talking about the key that opens the front door. I'm talking about the power to unlock a contract you thought had locked you up forever. The power and right to be free rather than bound. When you are free and you know it, you can live in your home to stay, or you can come and go as you please, without submitting your priorities to the fear of "the institution" that claims to control your life with a sheet of paper.

The bank may hold the paper, but you hold the house, you hold the key. In this book you will discover how to live in your own home for fun and profit. You will find a filebox full of recipes for taking back control of your mortgage. But the central secret of seizing the high ground and beating your banker to the punch, the secret that imbues the whole filebox of recipes, is the moral and legal right of nonpayment. Real estate law is now so complex that the right to be exempted from contractual mortgage obligation can be extended to almost anyone, in full accordance with the law of the land and in full harmony with your scruples.

When you control your mortgage, you control a major portion of your life: time is money. If you free up money from the mortgage category, there is no shortage of other responsible ways you can put that money to work. You can give yourself a sabbatical, invest in improving your house for once rather than watching it run down, start up a business or cottage industry, give to the needy, invest in precious metals and stocks, and of course spend a little on entertaining yourself. If you have the right (you usually do) and if the mortgage lenders are in the wrong (they very often are), you owe it to yourself to know the truth and to be prepared to make an informed decision.

No course of action is without risks; even staying in prison is risky. But when you've learned from this book how to take control of your mortgage and your life, I think you'll know whether there are nonpayment options that fit your situation and your style. Even if you decide that your situation is best served by striving until you reach that illusionary payoff number, you owe it to your friends and family to let them learn the revelations of this book, as I guarantee some of them will need to know their rights someday too.

In this book you'll not only find out how to qualify yourself, you'll also find out, step by step, how to protect yourself and your rights in your property from those who would disdain your legal rights, those who are secretly hoping you'll never find out what your rights are, the very rights described in this book. Banks love business as usual and they hate to admit any of the numerous exceptions that American legislators have built into the law to protect you, the homeowner. If you pay your mortgage, you won't get much attention from the banks. If you do not pay, yes, you will get attention from the banks. And if you assert your rights whenever you are called on to do so, believe me, you can make the banks -pay- attention.

You can get out of your mortgage free and start living in your dream home again. Without even moving. To learn more about the fine art of exempting yourself from mortgage payments and thwarting lenders and foreclosers while fully satisfying both courts and consciences, read chapter 1 now to get started, "It's Your Home."

Table of Contents

1. It's Your Home: Reclaim the High Ground

2. Get Out of Your Mortgage Free

3. How Far Can You Go By Yourself?

4. How Fast Can You Win Your Home Back?

5. Force Your Lender Back to the Table

6. Stand Your Ground

7. Call the Shots (I)

8. Call the Shots (II)

9. Frustrate Foreclosers

10. How We Left Debtors' Prison for Good

11. Take Courage and Stand Strong

Chapter 1

It's Your Home: Reclaim the High Ground

What is a mortgage anyway? How does it get put together? Let's put it this way: your stomach would turn less if I told you how sausage was made. The more certain you are of what you think a word means, the more you can learn by looking it up. Your trusty Merriam-Webster might give you a big shock if you hadn't heard it before. The word "mortgage" comes from the French word "mort," meaning dead. The bold type in the etymology suggests that, if we want further information about the word's history, there's "more at MURDER." Right after the mortgages in the dictionary, the next word is "mortician." After that, "mortification."

A mortgage is literally a dead "gage," or a dead pledge. It goes back to the feudal system, where a property was not conveyed to a person (the "vassal") until he "killed" the prior claim by making the specified payment. It's a death pact! And you unwittingly volunteered to be the murderer!

In this scientific day and age we don't settle for locking the poor landholding vassal who has been transplanted into our times into a single lump-sum payment, as of old. Oh, no. We have perfected the art of computerized calculation of compounded daily interest harmonized with an idealized decades-long perpetuity. This ensures the woebegone modern-day version of the medieval vassal makes not less than -four hundred eighty- payments in forty years. (More than double that if he pays biweekly, but that's not to knock biweekly payments.) The alleged benefit to the vassal, as he racks his brains to understand how these figures are calculated, is that each one of those hundreds of payments is as small as possible. Small, that is, considering that the interest he's paying would be enough to buy two or three additional houses beyond the one he's buying with principal, if only he could get all the money together at once.

This amazing miracle of compounded interest, where you are told to concentrate on a tiny number to distract you from the much larger number representing the cost of your house, and the number representing the interest profit that is much larger still, is called "amortization."

If you're sharp you saw our friend Mort there again. The French word "Amortization" comes from an old Latin word and it means "deadening" the mortgage. Apparently your monthly payment serves to make your mortgage number go just a little bit numb, and then just a little bit number. (It's a number number. Go figure.)

The banksters love ordinary processes because ordinary processes keep you from thinking about that insane usurious profit that they're making. Under ordinary processes, your mortgage won't be -dead- until the very end of its term.
Until then, your mortgage is -undead-!

If you're confused, let the experts try to explain it to you: go to this website: http://www.youtube.com/watch?v=dt2GtwhX8ho .

But enough about those zombies. Now here's the definition you are scanning this book for.

"Nonpayment," in mortgage law, is the invoking of the legal and moral right, in appropriate situations, to exempt oneself from literal fulfillment of an amortization. It's also called "debt repudiation." Sometimes it's more than a right, it's a responsibility. A debt can be repudiated for two basic reasons: either the creditor unjustly handled the debt, or the debtor justly declared a legal exemption. It's your right to exempt yourself when the law is on your side and your longterm plan calls for it. But it's your -responsibility- to question a debt when your creditor is in the wrong.

The right of nonpayment or repudiation is not limited to cases where courts have found creditor error or debtor exemption. It is a fundamental right that can be exerted by any of us if our mortgage is pursuing like a bloodsucking zombie while we've been minding our own business. Let me introduce you to a quick-fire list of additional definitions. Every one of these terms is a method for staying in your home on your own terms, and every one allows the right of nonpayment to be exerted until you get what you are negotiating for.

- "Forbearance," in real estate, is the same as temporary agreed nonpayment. The operative word is "temporary," as the lender assumes you will eventually pay the full amount plus interest (a greater amount than without the forbearance). A short-term hardship could lead you to request a forbearance for three or six months (the longest we've heard is three years); but in every case you have that unpaid debt remaining attached to your mortgage, whether your monthly payment is increased later or the term of your bondage is extended. For methods of nonpayment that don't require the lender to agree, read on.
- "Adverse possession" is the basic situation where your possession or occupation of a property is no longer deemed to be in the interests of your lender. This happens because of the lender's abuse or neglect of its interests (construed very broadly, it can include any failure to negotiate with you or keep you happy), which is an open door to nonpayment. The next few terms are methods
- "Loan modification" is an agreement for the lender to recalculate the mortgage in your favor based on intervening events and actuarial incentives. It is also called a "loan workout plan" or "mortgage restructuring."
- "Short sale," in real estate, means a sale to a buyer who recognizes that you're underwater and the property is appraised at less than what you currently owe on it. A short sale compels the lender to make concessions to protect its interests. While you should be prepared to move on to another property if the short sale is successful, the process can be long and your rights of nonpayment and occupation are preserved as long as it remains active.
- "Deed in lieu of foreclosure" is an agreement for the lender to retake ownership of the property, usually on the argument that a foreclosure would be much more costly to the lender. If it succeeds, you often remain in the property if you can make a lease payment indefinitely or for a known term.

- "Deficiency waiver," often attached to short sales and deeds in lieu, is an agreement that the amount you're underwater will be forgiven in consideration of the new transaction. To say it oversimplified, the difference between the property's value when you bought it and its current value is simply written off as debt forgiveness.
- Most people know what "foreclosure" is from old Scrooge McDuck cartoons, but they don't know that it is often a bad idea for the lender. A foreclosing lender is one who has decided to attempt to retake the property unilaterally. But in buyer-protective America, there are many ways to prevent lenders from taking this step in the first place or to prevent them from completing the process, which will encourage you as you read on. Oh, and, to restate the obvious, when you've had foreclosure filed against you, you almost always have a moral imperative not to throw good money after bad.

The rest of this book will teach you everything you need to know about nonpayment: When it's appropriate; How it's done; What it accomplishes; Why it works; Where to find help; and Who has used the right of nonpayment to their great advantage.

You can be next. After you've adopted the winning philosophy, learned the winning strategies, and navigated the winning path as described in this book, please write us using the contact information in the back of this book and you may be eligible to appear in a future edition.

Chapter 2

Get Out of Your Mortgage Free

Congresswoman Marcy Kaptur is on record speaking of the amazing results of homeowners learning the law and applying it to improve their conditions. But before you start seeing amazing results for yourself, you plan.

Maybe you've already "defaulted" by getting behind and not keeping monthly contact with your lender. Maybe you're keeping current only with creative accounting. Or maybe you're a great creditor but you only keep up your reputation by denying yourself everything else. That doesn't help much: if you can afford to keep the house but can't afford to keep anything in it, you're just as much enslaved to the mortgage as anyone else.

But you've never felt like you have any choice.

What are your choices? Whenever you face this question, always start from logic. Are you making it, or not? You have a basic average earning level each month, you have a basic average expense amount, and most of the time you already know whether you're treading water or whether you're really going under.

To fix a budget question, you have three choices. Increase earnings (get that second job?); decrease expenses (find a way to live on less?); or do nothing (accept responsibility for letting it get worse day after day).

But what if there is a clear, legal, and moral path to live on less by paying less mortgage? Or no mortgage?

To pay, or not to pay?

That is the question that you face. And you do have a choice. There is never a "can't," and there is never a "have to." There are always options.

We'll let you work on the options of generating extra revenue streams and of keeping debt serviced. We know you're reading this book because you want to be reassured that not paying your mortgage is a real option.

The answer is yes. In any basic situation there is always a legal path, fair to everyone that puts you in line to stop paying and keep staying.

Some situations are tougher than others, and not everyone will cooperate. But if they play by the rules, you can win. (If you happen to run into a cheater, you need to play a different game: close this book and get someone who knows the law.) In the ordinary course of dealing with law-abiding lenders, you can win. Because you get to decide what game to play and when to play it, and you get to move first and set the tempo that dictates the outcome.

You can decide whether to play on the fast track or the slow track. You can consider your options, make a hard decision today, and start directing the show tomorrow. Calling your own shots. Or you can consider your options and make a decision to give yourself more time to make the hard decision. Then you can start your legal stall tactics tomorrow. (Delay always sets you up for the possibility that you might find another more convenient place to stay, especially if you're on the market for one.) Particularly, delay puts you in the place where you don't have to commit or be locked in.

You can decide whether to hold on to your equity or use it as a bargaining chip. The investment you've made in your equity is your first store of value. You can hold it for a rainy day and keep the wolf from the door in the meantime. Or you can call the tune with your equity and direct your lender how to dance.

You have another store of value too: time is money, and every day that you're protecting yourself from being kicked out of your home, you're pocketing the value of that day. That means that as long as you're staying and not paying, you're collecting the equivalent of the daily mortgage costs you -would- have paid. That's called "squatter rent" and, believe it or not, it's becoming a significant rainy-day fund for people just like yourself who have discovered the secret of keeping their lenders away. If at all possible, keep the money you would have paid in savings or in investments, both for self-discipline and because it's a very valuable bargaining chip. If the lender asks for good-faith money later in the process, your savings (and any interest) would then be available to satisfy what the lender views as "delinquency." (If you're stuck diverting your house payment to other debts and ordinary self-control budgeting doesn't help, you'll want reasonable documentation proving to a suspicious auditor that your "missing" squatter rent was not frittered away.)

If you are underwater in more than one property, you can always rent to ease the burden, or sell at a loss. Sometimes a multiple homeowner will want to move so that the correct property is regarded as the "primary property," the one you want to hunker down in. While these options do not immediately solve the core problem of a mortgage, they do ease the burden when they are available.

Even if foreclosure has already been threatened or initiated, you can still jump right in on the right foot. You can choose whether to stall the foreclosure or to go for the win and demand that the forecloser "produce the note." And always challenge the legal sufficiency of any claim made by a forecloser. There are always options!

One more decision to make is your exit strategy. As we discovered, the whole point of being under a mortgage is to slay it. The modern method of killing one's mortgage by a thousand paper cuts is ineffective for most people. You can kill your mortgage by finding some way to equalize the money you can offer with the money the lender can accept as a settlement; or you can kill it by showing its illegality in court; or you can kill it by causing the lender to show institutional ignorance for so long that you have effective homestead rights by virtue of years of "squatting." But don't assume that nonpayment is a permanent lifestyle: it's always to be used as a road to where you want to go. Ask yourself: are you primarily interested in nonpayment because you want to have clearance to stay unmolested in your current home, or is it because you want to have time to find a better one? (I routinely lose this argument, but love for one's home is very sentimental and often stress-inducing, and finding a better purchase or rental is very liberating and often stress-relieving. Sometimes, fighting one semipermanent outcome, like foreclosure, means losing a battle against a different semipermanent outcome, like chronic fatigue. Make sure the victory isn't worse than the defeat.) When you know your exit strategy, you'll know what to do with your equity and squatter rent.

Decision Matrix
Use this checklist to determine which strategies you favor.

Alternatives to Nonpayment

- Am I keeping my eyes open at least monthly for alternate methods of increasing earnings or decreasing expenses?
- Am I actively seeking to sublease any unoccupied properties or rooms?
- Am I negotiating with other vendors and providers for lower rates on ordinary expenses?
- Am I making lifestyle changes as appropriate to my situation?

Nonpayment

- Am I convinced of my right to exempt myself from a defective loan? (For the very scrupulous, please see the next chapter.)
- Am I prepared to "read my lease" and take the responsibility to judge any defects?
- Am I holding sufficient equity to move forward?
- Am I going to be saving enough through "squatter rent" to be comfortable proceeding? (If not, you have other problems to solve too!)

Exit Strategy

- Am I currently living in the property I consider my primary home?
- Am I intending to keep my primary home in the endgame, or to be moved into a new primary home before the endgame?

Strategy Matrix

The primary benefit of each strategy when applied on either the fast track or the slow track is listed in the table below.

Strategy

- Fast track
- Slow track

Loan modification

- Seize any money the lender has "left on the table" at this instant.
- Convert any other holdings into equity in your primary home for longterm interest savings.

Short sale

- Find a buyer who is more fun to rent from than your lender is to mortgage from.
- Hold off your creditor by doing "due diligence" to sell even if the market is soft.

Deficiency waiver

- Take advantage of the lender's secret fears of the costs and time damage of foreclosure.
- By making a good-faith offering, take advantage of the lender's secret fears of vandalism and theft.

Naked deed in lieu

- Avoid outright foreclosure and its credit damage by settling quickly.
- A deed in lieu without deficiency waiver may be preferable if you need to absorb secondary liens.

Foreclosure

- When you're under the ultimate pressure, "demanding the note" can often deliver an outright win rapidly.
- Hold the moral high ground by demanding your rights and reparations to the very end, and deal out a surprise finish.

As you learn the strategies, come back to the checklist regularly to make sure you've made all your preparations and you have a first-string and second-string plan in mind that take best advantage of your strengths and goals according to the strategy matrix.

(Finally, there's one other option that we see very many people taking and that has occasional success, but we don't think it should be listed in this table. That option is called:

"DO NOTHING."
There are no absolutely no real benefits to inaction (or distraction tactics). The only apparent benefit is short-term psychological catharsis, and mature homeowners recognize that avoidance and "happification" doesn't last. You, of course, are already taking one of your best actions by continuing to read. But if you ever find yourself tempted to inaction, find something, anything, that makes a positive step forward: reread, call a friend, or throw out a lifeline. If analysis tempts you to paralysis, prevent yourself from getting stuck by taking some step even if you don't know which way forward is. Most people have at least occasional bouts of depression, and recognizing this will encourage you to take action with the greatest likelihood of achieving your goals.)

Chapter 3

How Far Can You Go By Yourself?

Are you scared yet? Or are you locked and loaded?

Many of the victory stories in this book were successfully carried out by individuals without specialized expertise. That's great for self-starters. But this chapter was written because not all of us are comfortable diving in suddenly. There is a good argument for enlisting the support of "trained professionals."

You don't necessarily need a professional to get most things done in life. This book was not written to give "professional advice." Professional advice is good for dotting t's and crossing i's. And sometimes vice versa. But professionals are basically just people who have studied a core set of practices and statements (a "profession") very closely. The services they offer to the public are generally consultative and consist of sharing the profession's knowledge and recommended applications with the public. Specialization.

If you are ready to move forward now, then skip to the next chapter. But if you are concerned about getting professional approval, read on. There are two basic rules of thumb for using professionals.

First, is the solution worse than the problem? That is, decide which would you rather spend: the -money- for the professional to render an opinion, or the -time- to research on the internet and come to your own conclusion. If you have enough money freed up and it's easy to find a lawyer, accountant, or broker, go ahead and enlist him or her to your cause. If you have more time on your hands, like a lot of our e-book readers, consider whether the steps involved below are worth your time, especially in the simpler questions, or whether you would rather punt and hand the ball off to someone else.

Second, is the professional your servant or your master? That is, establish first and foremost in the relationship that the professional's role is to give the advice and your role is to make the final decision. This will surprise the person you are paying, who may not be as used to working hard for a living as you are. But you won't regret it later when the professional disagrees with you and gives you all the potential downsides for your preference, and you want to go ahead anyway. The professional's job is to protect you against pitfalls, not to make matters go easily for the professional.

Let me teach you some lawyerspeak. When a lawyer says, "You have to," it means, "I can avoid doing any more hard thinking about your case if you do." When a lawyer says, "The law says," it means, "I don't want to take time to tell you how people get around this one." When a lawyer says, "It's too late," it means, "I don't want to take time to tell you how people get around this one." When a lawyer says, "Use this form," it means, "I forget the details but I do know that by telling you to fill out every line I've absolved myself of my legal responsibility." Get it? It's the classic path of least resistance, and it counts on you not to resist.

Ask probing questions of your professional to ensure that you get the answers you want and need. Stick to the topic and don't be distracted by nonanswers.

When I start contracting with a professional, I give a standard spiel that clarifies my role straight up. I explain that the professional is providing a service and I am providing the pay for the service. That means I have the right to decide how services will be conducted, I have the right to have my questions answered, I have the right to accept or reject advice, and I have the right to make final decisions about my interests after knowing the upside and downside to each option. The professional has the right to express a professional opinion very strongly, but does not have the right to override my legal decisions.

I tell this to my doctors, lawyers, consultants, accountants, whomever will listen. Not all of them do. This weeds out those who call themselves professionals but who have difficulty remaining professional when someone disagrees with them. If their services will be unable to survive a simple disagreement with a client, it's better to test that from the start.

Once you've taken responsibility for these two decisions, choosing whether to spend your own time or to spend your money on someone else's time, and then choosing to take responsibility for how you act on the advice rather than leave the responsibility to the professional, you are ready to consider your case more specifically. Let's start with lawyers because they're so easy to pick on.

When do you need a lawyer?

You will want a lawyer if you are a big-picture thinker rather than a detail-type thinker. The law is a labyrinth and should be threaded only by those who are willing to adapt to the detail-oriented thinking necessary. Of these two basic personality types, if you favor big-picture thinking, if you enjoy the executive overviews and leave the footnotes to others, the only time you want to navigate the law yourself is when you need to know the answers in such detail that it's better to self-adapt your personality type than to delegate the task to another.

You may want a lawyer if your case deals with extra complexity. If there are corporate or estate considerations and multiple parties connected to your property, you will need to weigh your ability to research and analyze all the appropriate laws, against your need to prioritize other activities.

You may want a lawyer if you need the intimidation factor: even when one letter contains the same legalese as another, if one bears a letterhead with a couple professional abbreviations (P.A.) that represent more clout and association power than the other, it is responded to with kid gloves rather than with brass knuckles. Paying a bar member solely for what he or she is, and for what that means to others, may sound inequitable even while it remains efficacious.

You may want a lawyer if you already have a working relationship with one on a given property. Usually, with a lawyer who knows the history of your property, you have already "paid to get in" and you can leverage that person's services to get the best advice. On the other hand, if you are underwater or in difficulty partly due to the advice of your lawyer, that may be a good sign that it is time to reevaluate your relationship and determine if you are getting the service you need!

You may want a lawyer if you want a specialist in one of the methods described in later chapters. Your local bar association will have recommendations.

If you've read the disclaimer to this book, you know that we protected ourselves by telling our readers that, if they are so irresponsible as to take this book as anything more than simple information presented at the reader's own risk, they definitely need to consult a lawyer.

Often your situation is simple enough that you can hire a paralegal in lieu of a lawyer. An independent paralegal is certified to perform all the logistics tasks that a lawyer does, often has comparable experience to a lawyer, and is almost always cheaper. The primary difference is that a lawyer has full latitude to represent you and has a fiduciary duty to look out for your interests, such as in court, while paralegals perform the majority of clerical work for their clients (whether lawyers or individuals) but do not have professional liability protection. Often a trained specialist paralegal is all you need.

If your plan is simple and you can handle the legalese, then make your own decision. But either way, be proactive and be responsible: invest the time and money that is necessary to make the right decision for your property, and commit to the risks and consequences before you invest. It's important to stick with your decision, because changing it in midstream requires more investment.

We wish you well!

When do you need a Certified Public Accountant?

You will want a Certified Public Accountant (CPA) if you are a people-oriented thinker rather than a task-oriented thinker, or a right-brained thinker rather than a left-brained thinker. You don't need to be a logic maven to know when you don't like math and want to delegate it to someone else. On the other hand, the accounting you need doesn't rely on advanced math as much as ensuring you haven't neglected any money movements, which is more of a logic task.

If you already do your own taxes yearly or quarterly, then you won't be surprised by the accounting involved in property negotiation. If at some point you previously turned your taxes over to a CPA, there's someone you can approach. Most of the proposals in this book are easier than calculating annual taxes.

If you have several properties or rentals, you might need an accountant just to manage them. But the primary virtue of a certified public accountant is his or her ability to document transactions in accord with generally accepted accounting principles. So it's up to you whether you want bulletproof documentation, or if you're not moving that many buckets of water around.

The principles involved in this book are much simpler than "generally accepted accounting principles." You're free to make your own decision not to involve a CPA.

Let me encourage you to set aside time to take one particular step involving talking with accountants, and that step is to get intimate with your credit report. A credit report is a composite of the opinions of accountants and actuaries at the three primary credit bureaus (Equifax, Experian, and TransUnion) as to your economic history. What's important is that, according to federal law, these accountants already work for you in a limited sense, because they have fiduciary duties they must carry out whenever you ask.

This point hardly needs a step-by-step because there is so much data available about how to get it done. You can call 1-800-FACT-ACT 1-800-FACT-ACT or use any of the online sources to obtain the report, and you are allowed a new free report every year (just don't pay a middleman unless there are additional services needed that you are really confident you would rather not handle yourself). Then you follow the instructions to dispute any problematic entries and ensure your comments appear on the record. This can be done at your convenience and only takes a couple hours, and it is very useful later anytime your lender wants to make objections.

Whatever lenders may be saying about their own inerrancy, homeowners have actually tested them on their recordkeeping and have regularly uncovered a sorry history of erratic documentation. I know people who have been completely passed over because of false and misleading information in the lender's copy of the credit report. The lender's negotiator relies on a computer's algorithmic interpretation of your report and may, for instance, be trusting in a completely bogus number for your debt as a percentage of earnings. The whole approval decision can and may hinge on a single (wrong) entry. Always question where spurious data came from and get answers: it takes the negotiator off balance.

If the credit bureau put the mistake in your report, they are required by law to fix it any time you dispute it. If the bureau had it right and the lender has made the mistake, you can use their error when the topic comes up in negotiation. By having your correct copy ready, you hold the high ground and have an easy "turkey shoot" when it comes to defeating their mistaken assumptions.

And let me give you a word about one group of accounting employees that I can confidently say you almost never need to talk to: namely, collectors. Case law is so favorable to debtors that you have zero technical reasons to talk to collectors and very few other reasons. You have the power to ignore all print and electronic mail, to screen all calls that identify as obscure acronyms or vague financial-sounding companies, and to give the standard do-not-call speech when you are accidentally reached (that speech is "please put this number on the do-not-call list," which all call center employees are trained to respond to with a polite disclosure paragraph and immediate disconnect). There are excellent boilerplate response letters (search for information on the Fair Debt Collection Practices

Act) that dispute all claims and demand all rights. Collectors that threaten damage to your credit report are best handled via the credit agency, -not- the creditor, as already stated. Only in the case of threats of liens and judgments do collectors have any unilateral power, and in those cases you (or a professional representative) should engage in the lender's administrative process for response and resolution, which usually involves a different department than collections. Hierarchically, upon receiving a request for counterprocess, collection staff are expected either to transfer you to the proper department (e.g., to delinquency customer service), or to suspend collections while handling the administrative process themselves. To be sure, it's very important to run toward rather than away from your lender, and to overcommunicate: but that should almost always be done with other personnel than the collection staff themselves.

When do you need a certified Realtor or other real estate professional?

"Realtor" is a brand name of the real estate trade industry association, the National Association of Realtors. Some people now call themselves "realtors" without having a trade membership, but they may be professionals anyway based on education, experience, or other affiliation. The first question for real estate brokers is who licenses them and what that license is worth.

You may want a real estate broker if you are more task-oriented than people-oriented. The agent or broker has the ability and network to find buyers and sellers, and the networking time that an agent will put in for you does have its value. So if you choose a plan where finding a willing third party is necessary and you need someone with people skills, an agent is a good choice.

You will want a real estate broker if you need a good negotiator. If you enter an agency agreement, the real estate broker will have a fiduciary duty to ensure that your needs are met and that prices are reasonable. Knowledge of appraisals and marketing will help the broker serve you better, and the broker's personal network will probably include contact personnel and knowledge of departments within lender organizations that will help you choose among options and presentations. Make sure you know whether the broker has entered an agency agreement with any sellers, as this affects your own agency agreement.

You can also hire a real estate broker without an agency agreement. This means that the broker is merely working to connect a buyer and a seller together, sometimes without a commission, and is ensuring understanding and compliance with law to complete the transaction properly. In some states, like Florida, it is illegal for the broker to be an agent both of the buyer and of the seller, due to potential conflict of interest, so "transaction brokerage" is the preferred arrangement under the laws of such states.

As with lawyers, many real estate brokers specialize in the methods described in this book. You can always find these people because they advertise heavily on Google. Finding a -superior- specialist who will work with you and for you is a bigger challenge, of course.

Often you can find a nonprofit or charitable housing counseling agency that helps people negotiate the complexities of real estate law without being involved in the transactions themselves. Like a broker, a housing counselor often already has relationships with lender personnel who may have already helped other homeowners with their successes.

If you're working with such real estate professionals, make sure to contact them to help prepare or review packages you intend to present to lenders, or to get information from lenders that seem recalcitrant in giving internal data to you.

While many of the broker's or counselor's services are potentially doable "by owner," the real answer to the question of whether to involve a professional comes down to whether you want to be the one responsible for doing those things, or whether you want to be responsible to delegate them.

When do you need the support of someone else?

There is one other group of people whom you may need to enlist for assistance: family, friends, and spiritual support. There is no substitute for having strong relationships in your personal life to carry you through the process of reclaiming your home. Some situations require standing your ground for years and that requires a moral compass and a support network.

To this question, we would say that all of us need support in our lives. The degree to which you'll need to lean on your friends and family depends mostly on the complexity and longevity of the path you choose based on your circumstances. But having a caring spouse or intimate friend will allow you the chance to validate and strengthen your strategy with a fellow planner.

Having a spiritual counselor will help you with any questions of scruple. We are hopeful that we have covered all the legal bases in these pages, and no one would counsel you to break the law, but we know there's a higher principle at work too. Not breaking the law is just part of not betraying your conscience. In this book you will find out the laws that exempt you from payment of a contract you signed with your own hand, and there are quite a few. But it's even more important to be sure your -conscience- has signed on to your new plan as well.

To this we would say: "natural law" should be reflected by civil law. If the law permits you to take adverse possession of a home after a period of time, it happens because lawmakers believe it is the right way for a law-abiding citizen to perfect a claim to a home when a seller or lender has broken the contract by failing a duty in a notorious way first. When one person breaks a contract, the other party to the contract is no longer bound by it; it's broken. Plain and simple. Let it go.

On the other hand, it's a free country, and it's a very godly choice to regard the contract as not broken out of a principle of forgiveness, and to continue to pay on it. Some people just have a "call" to do this, and we wouldn't stop you if you're one of those people. This world is such that people find ways to fulfill their callings. But in any case, choose a trustworthy spiritual counselor to discuss the matter with. Out of all the people out there who give free advice, the religious man ought to be the best advisor!

It's very important to be fully onboard with a plan when you are in a big sharkpool like the real estate world. We want you to be equipped with the tools you need not only to make the decision quickly but also to know you can stick with it through the long haul. Once your heart and soul are set on your course, nobody can stop you.

Chapter 4

How Fast Can You Win Your Home Back?

Now the time has come to review your options and then make your decision. Let me share a little art of war with you. One way of defeating an enemy is to go for the jugular, to attack the exposed weak point and win decisively. But another way of defeating an enemy is often more effective but less appreciated: conserve yourself while watching and using the enemy's weakness against him. An overbearing, bulky enemy may make a misstep and be overturned by a timely application of asymmetrical force in a moment that has been carefully harvested. When you are watching for either approach, your background knowledge of the enemy and the immediate opportunity will dictate which kind of victory you achieve.

How do you watch and win?

Before you make any moves that would commit you to a particular approach, remember the basics. You may have heard that in any challenge relating to any person, organization, or situation, you always have the basic "three options." You can work to change the challenging person, organization, or situation; you can work to put distance between yourself and the challenge; or you can work to change yourself, and to change your ability not to be challenged. Always review all three options, don't "foreclose" any of them.

If the situation is the payment requirements of a mortgage, you can change how the mortgage is to be paid, distance yourself from paying the mortgage, or change the claim that you are "unable" to pay and find a way to slay the mortgage once and for all, with your own or other people's money.

The three options

1. **Change the Mortgage.** This means the large overhanging debt remains but the nature of the obligation has changed in some way that works for your budget and situation. One way

to change the mortgage is to change the -terms- bilaterally with the lender through a loan modification. During a modification process, you can renegotiate, or make specific proposals like a principal reduction or a reverse mortgage. Another method of change is to change the -lender-. Your current lenders may be quite willing to take you off their hands if another private or public party will step in to take on the risk of holding your mortgage. One way to do this is through a short sale package. Of course if the problematic property is vacant and you find a renter, you have also fundamentally changed the mortgage in the short term by changing the -occupier-, though you still bear the responsibility of slaying the beast in due time by ensuring the rest of the mortgage term is fulfilled whether or not your renter continues to work out.

2. **Use Distance.** This means responsibly separating yourself from the duty of ensuring regular payments. The primary method is called "adverse possession," a protected legal status that means you continue to possess your property, but you have explicitly notified your noteholder that their inactivity or abusive behavior has been adverse to their interests in retaining the note. While you do this, in many cases it's a good idea to continue paying a small amount ($5, $10, or $20) each pay period to demonstrate that -you- are not neglecting your responsibilities; however, in some cases, you might be advised not to make any payments, in order to protect your legal position in particular cases.

3. **Change Your Abilities.** This is the superhero option, where you come out and reveal that you've always had more sovereign power than your secret identity ever told anyone. It does require belief in your ability and clarity in your conscience. But -we- know you can do it. The first method is to change your ability to hold on to your property: finding another place to live with superior terms allows you to present your current lender with a deed in lieu of foreclosure. You can do this with or without a "deficiency waiver," meaning that the lender forgives ("waives") the amount by which you're "underwater," which a lender might do just to be rid of you. (This is pretty much the same as "short selling"

back to the lender.) Then there's the method that really lets you out of the phone booth: it's called "demanding the note."

When you demand that the lender produce the note of your indebtedness in court, you shift the burden of proof off yourself and onto the lender. The alleged "noteholders" are more afraid of this strategy than they let on, because the fractionating and reassignment associated with most big loans from big banks makes it impossible to demonstrate a chain of custody of your note that satisfies the rules of evidence. In the last several years, and particularly after the end of Lehman Brothers, banks have been shoveling their failed commercial paper into bigger and bigger messes, faster and faster, to ensure that the auditors never see whichever room currently contains the mess. Your house may presently be securing a trillion-dollar derivatives bet on whether some Eastern European country will go bankrupt or not. In the process, banks have been shown to fail to keep all their documents clean as regards the history of any one particular mortgage (yours).

And banks are much much more heavily regulated than we little homeowners are. Ouch.

So shifting the burden creates a strong likelihood that your lender will be told, "your papers are not in order." I don't know about you, but I'd much rather put that risk on the other party than on myself. With a little preparation, demanding the note is the "nuclear option" of homesteaders in the 21st century.

The next choice you have to make is whether to go for the jugular yourself immediately, or whether to wait and use your lender's weaknesses to slay your mortgage. That is, you can use a fast track or a slow track.

Why might you want a fast track?

You want to attempt a fast track if any of the "indicator lights" suggest openness to a quick resolution that meets your needs.

- If the lender is approachable, or if other lenders are advertising lower rates than your current one, these are signals to propose a loan modification or a principal reduction.
- If you're over 62, a reverse mortgage is also available.
- If the property is vacant, compare your costs (mortgage, utilities, taxes and insurance, and any association fees) with the average rental in the area to see if renting is workable. A real estate professional can help you find out the comparables or register you for internet resources that can keep you posted.
- If the market favors selling at a discount, you may be able to find a buyer quickly and submit a short sale package to your lender asking that the sale be completed at a value lower than the amount you then owe.
- If the lender appears to be threatening to foreclose but has not done so, you can offer a deed in lieu of foreclosure, with a deficiency waiver. This delays the foreclosure and interests the lender in not giving your credit report such a negative hit. A deed in lieu assumes that you are not working with your primary property or that you will have a place to go.
- If the lender has difficulty with a deficiency waiver, you can remove the waiver as a bargaining chip and offer a "naked" deed in lieu. The difference is that you will probably have a note after the deed in lieu, requiring you to make a small monthly payment to satisfy the difference in addition to whatever new living expenses you have. The math can still work out.
- If you are able to argue your case well in court, or you know someone who is able to, then you can proceed with demanding the note proving your (alleged) indebtedness. This has even worked in the worst case, where foreclosure proceedings have been initiated. If you are under the barrel, it may be time to make the attempt.

However, if none of these situations seem to apply, circle the wagons, hunker down, and prepare for the long haul.

Why might you want a slow track or "delay track?"

The purpose of the slow track is to delay and protect yourself until you figure out what you want to do.

- Sometimes, the situation changes and one or more of the "indicator lights" goes on suddenly: if you are watching for these events, you will be ready to jump to the fast track and get the victory you desire. The lender may change, the market may change, you might reach that age of 62 that the Department of Housing and Urban Development finds so sacred for getting a reverse mortgage started.
- Sometimes, you can initiate a process (like looking for a buyer) and have reasonable expectation that the process will be completed but without any idea when. Planning to be on the slow track before you start will keep you strong for the time it takes to complete the transaction and reach the goal.
- And, most important, the longer you possess the house, the better the likelihood that it will become yours by "adverse possession." Because this is a key plank in the strategy, a few words more are appropriate.

When your possession of the property is no longer in the lender's interests, it is considered "adverse" to those interests. It can easily become adverse because of the lender's own abuse or neglect of the mortgage. For instance, if you have asked for improvements or concessions because of property damage (arising from the property's age, from local crime, or other reasons), the lender has an interest in resolving your demand, and neglecting this resolution is contrary or "adverse" to its interests. If you have asked for any change in the mortgage before due to changing circumstances (whether it's because people realized that sellers were gouging them by charging extra for a mortgage bubble, or because your boss is an idiot who won't pay you enough because of fears spurred by those who are misregulating the economy), your lender has an interest in resolving that demand as well.

Lenders are not required to give in to every demand their tenants make. But they are under the gun because of their legal responsibility to domicile you "reasonably." Billions of dollars of litigation occur over what is "reasonable" and, unless they can send a clear-cut refusal letter within 30 days with a bulletproof legal argument, every demand can be litigated at least in theory. And that makes them afraid, very afraid. Any issue they don't resolve promptly might be held later to prove that they didn't take "reasonable" care of "their" property.

The legal and moral argument for adverse possession is that if you don't take care of something for long enough and someone else does, you really can't claim that it's yours anymore. Possession is nine-tenths of the law.

The law has recognized this since about the 11th century. In those days, British and other European landholders were anxious to have their ownership of land recorded in the government's archives, and books of "titles" to real estate were created. The problem was that, later on, if you knew your family owned the land a hundred years ago but couldn't maintain it and someone else moved in and did maintain it (or "squatted" there), the law needed to decide whether the age-old "title" to the land was valid, or whether the "sweat equity" of the property's maintainer was more valid. Rival families got to arguing about the meaning of old transactions and old "understandings." In America, the Hatfields and McCoys were a notorious case of similar battles over competing claims of possession. Eventually a statute of limitations was set for property ownership claims. Nowadays it's generally ten years.

This is why we're hearing more about "urban squatters" who simply select a vacant mansion, more or less at random, and move in. They have little to lose in the worst case (going on the lam and doing the same thing in the next block or next state); and they have much to gain if their occupation is uncontested. While random occupation is generally lawless, the fact is that landowners who do not maintain their property do impair their own interests. And if you have some legitimate tie to the property, urban squatting might be defensible.

At any rate, if you can stay in your current residence for ten years after the initial date of any act of disinterest by the alleged titleholder, you have every possibility and hope of being given the title later as the adverse possessor. That means, however many years ago your first episode of disagreement with the lender occurred, you can deduct that from the ten years.

The six traditional legal requirements of proving adverse possession are remembered by using the mnemonic phrase "AN ECHO." This phrase stands for the following:

- **Actual:** You are using the property the same way an owner would as typical for the local area.
- **Notorious:** You are providing the titleholder with sufficient notice of potential impairment.
- **Exclusive:** The titleholder is -not- using the property over the period that you are using it.
- **Continuous:** You are physically present as often as an owner would be, without being ejected.
- **Hostile:** Your occupation and claim lacks full permission and is adverse to titleholder interest.
- **Open:** Your use of the property is reasonably visible, such as by use of signs, gates, or fences.

It is important to establish the initial date of adverse possession to notify the lender or bank of the origin of -your- rightful claim on the property due to its lapse in attention to its interests.

If you have decided to take the slow track because you don't have a "quick win" potential situation, then one of your first steps will be to write an initial hardship letter and declare adverse possession to have begun. Most of the traditional requirements will have been met simply by your living where you do. The requirement of "hostile" or adverse occupation is met by finding the date at which you first informed the lender of any significant problem with the property that was not immediately resolved, or the date at which you were first late or deficient in a payment.

Writing a hardship letter may appear impossible without a form, but in this case writing from your own experience is better. The initial letter can always be improved later and any errors corrected. Your initial hardship letter should have the following elements.

1. The claim of hardship itself: state the circumstances that compel nonpayment. If your budget makes it impossible to pay the mortgage and other reasonable obligations without accumulating monthly debt, that is a claim of financial hardship (often called "can't pay"). If the lender has not addressed property problems in the past that compel your nonpayment as the rightful response to ensure your concerns are addressed, or if you have evidence the lender engaged in predatory practices, that is a claim of lender repudiation (also called "won't pay"). Document your claim of hardship (medical records, a layoff letter from an employer, news or court reports about the lender's legal troubles, a divorce decree, changes to an adjustable-rate mortgage, or even an invoice for replacing a costly air conditioning system).
2. Goodwill: If you are willing to pay a nominal monthly amount up to $20 to express "goodwill" in the hardship circumstances, say so: and then don't miss any such payment unless your particular path requires evidence of a period of time of total nonpayment. Making goodwill payments demonstrates that, while you disagree with being held a slave to an arbitrary chimera of demands, you still deign to recognize the diplomatic virtue of maintaining a relationship with the monster's owners. Usually goodwill maintains a record of monthly contact but also does not affect legal processes that rely on fixing delinquency periods. But, if you are going cold turkey and deciding on total nonpayment, say so, and then for your protection don't ever send a cent again until you have total resolution. Whether you are paying goodwill or not, ask your lender to commit mercifully not to report your delinquency to credit bureaus: this is in the lender's interest because they want to work with you to increase the likelihood of repayment, and, if you tell them which plan you want to propose to achieve that, they know that you're serious about working with them as well.
3. Adverse possession: You should state the initial date and circumstance that began adverse possession and memorize

and hold to that date whenever the topic comes up. (About the only reason to change the date of an adverse possession claim is if an attorney's research into the history, or your own later research, suggests sufficient reason for you to change it: don't change it based on lender demands or threats, but hold to what you know is right.) You should clearly explain why the event constituted a demonstration that the titleholders acted contrary to their own interests in retaining clear title to "their" property as a reasonable owner should have done. List any other examples of acting against interests, and conclude by tying in your nonpayment as the final demonstration of continuing adverse possession.

In short, if you see that one of the fast tracks is indicated by your situation, skip to that chapter and see if you can achieve your goals immediately. If you believe you will need a longer time (possibly years) to accomplish your preferred method of reclaiming title to your own home, then prepare to inform the lender via an initial hardship letter, and read the whole book thoroughly.

Even on the slow track you should -not- delay informing the lender of changes in your legal position beyond two to four weeks' notice, so either way you will want to make the first step in your plan -this month-. And you will want to ensure that you service your plan -every month- thereafter: don't just ride a wave of silence if you don't know where it will crash. The best way to preserve -your- rights, and not to get caught in the lender's trap of failing to secure its own property interests, is for you to start establishing a record of monthly documented attention to the mortgage problem. When you're paying a mortgage, that record is automatic. When you stop paying and when your nonpayment draws attention to you, it is essential that you (and your lawyer if any) have a continuous documented track of due diligence in carrying out your plan.

Make your call

Review the methods and rationales behind the tools described in this book. Use the list below to determine what chapter to read next.

Review your lender paperwork. Get an idea of exactly where they consider the mortgage to be. We hope that you've thrown all your letters from the lender into the same pile (and that it's not the trashbin). If you've at least looked at and attempted to understand every letter the lender has sent, even the collections letters, you've been given sufficient information on any point that the law requires you to be told. Lenders are not allowed to throw curveballs. If the monthly mail scares you or you've thrown out a lot of it, you or your broker might need a fast reconnaissance project to get yourself up to speed if you want to take advantage of a fast-track option. Be prepared to duplicate any documents you send the lender and to keep your file organized from here on out.

Interview your lender if necessary. You might need to remember call-center navigation techniques: always try to talk to a live person, even if the only option is the sales department. Dialing zero, or dialing nothing at all, often works. You might need to talk to two, or five, low-level employees before you find a decisionmaker, especially if you get automatically routed to collections. Be bold and ask for the department that deals with one of the strategies you are interested in; these departments have widely varying names, often "loss mitigation," or "foreclosure prevention" or "customer saves" or "loan resolution." Be prepared in case an hourly employee (or the supervisor of one) requires you to present formfill data in exchange for routing you to loss mit; know in advance whether you are ready to share your financial information, whether you need to talk to the specialist first, or whether you just need basic answers that your lender would appear unreasonable to refuse.

The key in this interview call is that you, or your representative, obtain the basic data about where the mortgage stands and how complex it is. But you might also be surprised to find that the lender is motivated to seek you out to apply for a particular process (such as loan modification) just because of internal or government incentives to improve their own bottom line! Sometimes the lender will even coach you on exactly what they need to approve your application. Approach the lender for the basics, and then take whatever else comes as gravy.

Review the basic decisions with your spouse, friend, or counselor. Pick your favorite and second favorite outcomes from among the options you've reviewed.

Once you know what plan will work best for you, go through step by step and work the plan. Keep an eye on circumstances that may change the plan. It's excellent advice to divide your efforts several ways, but give each of them proper treatment: don't switch horses in midstream. If you've started on a path and you need to continue on it for conscience's sake, see it through and don't sweat the temptations to alter course. Remember that you made the decision in the first place. And remember this: -any- plan will eventually work out if you are not slack in working it. The cosmos favors seekers of diligence.

As to specific strategies, loan modifications and variations are discussed in chapter 5, "Force Your Lender Back to the Table."

Short sales are the topic of chapter 6, "Stand Your Ground."

If you need to offer a deed in lieu, see chapters 7-8, "Call the Shots."

Chapter 9, "Frustrate Foreclosers," reveals the surprise moves that remain even in the worst cases.

Take a breather before diving into the strategies themselves in these coming chapters and set your mind and spirit on the goal and its achievability.

Chapter 5

Force Your Lender Back to the Table

Any renegotiation with your current lender to change terms in your favor falls in the category of loan modifications. Mods vary from simple to quite complex. What they all have in common is that they bring your lender to the table and force a consideration of, and a response to, your grounds for nonpayment. They also allow you a significant timeframe to retain your house without risk because the lender is staying within an amicable and well-defined administrative process.

Often nonpayment is a bridge to payment on much better terms. Sometimes it is a tactic during a modification in case the process goes bad and a threat of adverse possession needs support. In general, though, a modification is expected by the lender to result in restarting regular payments later, and it should be offered in good faith with this in mind. If the objection to nonpayment is "can't pay" rather than "won't pay," modification is recommended.

While the industry and the government has created a streamlined loan modification process, before we discuss it we should consider some related sideline processes separately. While these technically also modify the loan, they don't require full lender consideration of a modification.

Fast-track alternatives to the streamlined modification process

- Refinancing is a simplified modification that usually affects only the interest rate (resulting in slightly lower monthly payments). It is widely advertised because the refinancer has little work to do (computer amortization is very speedy), but has the benefit of a new loan (often "stolen" from the original lender). Often the new loan is an entirely rewritten version of essentially the same terms and the former lender is paid off. This means a first line of attack can be to tell your current lender you're considering switching to a better refi offer, one that you've found by searching for advertising or by speaking to your local Realtor. Refinance was more popular until about 2009 or 2010 because of lower interest rates and has become harder today. But a real estate professional in your confidence can help you find refinance options and loan programs beyond those generally advertised. In the easier cases, when all you need is to fend off the compound-interest monster by weakening its power, your original lender might heed your threat and agree to calculate a refinance quickly without too much paperwork, especially if your equity is over 15% or 20% or if they are earning fees for collecting refinances.

If so, congratulations! The lender left some money on the table and you found it. But this is only a first move in the gameplan you are considering, and you may be able to score with another method, even if the lender has already refinanced your loan.

- Forbearance, repayment plans, and equity loans are all tantamount to borrowing from yourself. Forbearance is the same as temporary agreed nonpayment, with the operative word being "temporary," as the lender assumes you will eventually pay the full amount plus interest (a greater amount than without the forbearance). A repayment plan works similarly but is the term used when there has already been significant past nonpayment: that is, it's forbearance used retroactively. An equity loan is getting a second lender to agree to loan you money against the -part- of your house that you "own," at least in theory.

In every case you have that unpaid debt remaining attached to your mortgage, whether your monthly payment is increased later or the term of your bondage is extended. These options do work well for self-employed and other people whose earnings are variable and who can expect to have a good year sooner or later even if they are having a difficult year now.

The key is knowing that you can afford to pay off both the original mortgage and the additional borrowing. If the original mortgage was entered into responsibly and you can enter into another contract with good business acumen, you might obtain and successfully repay such an arrangement. Partial or full forbearance, in particular, is often used because another process (loan modification, short sale approval) is pending and payback is anticipated when it closes.

However, if you're scouting around for loose money because the original mortgage has always been a questionable risk, -don't borrow from yourself!- Don't modify the loan in a way that merely postpones a repayment and keeps the mortgage "undead" for a longer period of time or with greater total payments. Because of its short-term approach, forbearance is actually the lenders' favorite option when they are asked to call the shots. (Don't ask them. Either decide that you're a good risk to borrow from yourself, or proactively choose a better option.) You never want an option that sets you up to fail, and, yes, some lenders have been shown to be unscrupulous enough to set up their borrowers to fail via unreasonable repayment pipe dreams.

To determine if repayment options are useful, get documents indicating that there was a significant hardship (current earnings statements, medical records, accident or damage reports, etc.) and that it was a one-time occurrence not likely to recur (prior earnings, professional medical opinion, appraisals, etc.). These will be primary documents used to persuade the lender that the amount is intended to be repaid: first see if they persuade you and your broker, and only try them out on the lender afterward. Of course, if you are invoking the right of nonpayment, or considering bankruptcy, we repeat, -don't complicate matters by borrowing your own money!- Whatever short-term benefit derives from one side (cash on hand) is zeroed by the other side (loss of equity) and further disadvantaged by the interest payments and the complication factor: such a transaction should only be engaged in if you're shrewd enough to recognize and manage all the risks in addition to your current mortgage. For the rest of us, it's better to use equity as a bargaining chip instead, such as for a streamlined loan modification or a short sale package.

- Mortgage insurance, if you purchased it as part of your loan, allows you to request that the insurer cover a payment deficit. In practice, however, this often works the same as forbearance or repayment, but with yet another company biting into the pie. (When it's not needed on a particular loan, the insurer gets paid for doing nothing; and when it is brought kicking and screaming into being convinced that it is "needed," the insurer releases only enough of its own money to keep its profit margins up. But this book isn't about insurance.) If the insurance company requires later repayment, then take "borrowing from yourself" seriously and decide whether you really are a good risk for the loan, knowing yourself as nobody else does!

- Reverse mortgages are generally available for homeowners over 62 to obtain value for the equity they have previously invested in (contact your real estate professional about exceptions to the age requirement). Arranging a reverse mortgage to protect your ability to remain at home can solve the root problem quickly, but it does have its own issues. The basic idea is that a second agreement is set up on top of your mortgage to pay back to you the amount of equity principal you paid in (not the interest, of course, which is always the majority of what you paid in!). The property remains in your name, but it's no more "yours" than when you live there under an active mortgage: the agreement requires the property to revert to the payor upon a qualifying event (you move out, you die, you pay back the amount reversed to you, etc.).

The good news is that you generally get to stay home indefinitely, sometimes the rest of your life, and that you get some value back on your principal (the interest is gone forever, as in any mortgage). The bad news is manifold. First, when the qualifying event occurs, the property immediately goes to the payor rather than you or your heirs. Second, the payor usually intends to sell the property to satisfy the unpaid balance, plus intervening interest, on the first mortgage! Guess who takes the full brunt of the risk of devaluation: if the sale doesn't pay for the mortgage balance and its new interest, you or your heirs are assessed for the difference. Third, the payor has a conflict of interest, as they gain no value while you live in your home to a ripe old age, so they have no interest in helping you set up or service the agreement, or explaining their payment plan in any detail. Fourth, when your equity runs out, the payments to you run out, which is not helpful if you were using them as a form of retirement pension. Fifth, you are still responsible for maintaining property insurance, homeowner's association fees, utilities, upkeep, and all other typical payments, all on behalf of the payor who gave you your principal back with such apparent generosity.

It's true that for some people a reverse mortgage can solve the basic problem of staying home without paying your mortgage. It worked for Jeanne Calment, who obtained her retirement home in France from her grandson under a form of reverse mortgage, where he was to receive the property as his own retirement home upon her death. Unfortunately for him, Calment refused to die and ultimately became the Guinness World Records oldest person in the world at age 122, and her grandson and other heirs predeceased her. Entre nous, be cautious not to set up a rivalry among family members that makes living long into the best revenge.

All in all, a reverse mortgage requires an iron will and cautious preparation, both financially and relationally. The payoffs are all weighted in the direction of the lender's benefit and there is significant and documented risk of the temptation of elder abuse (physical and psychological). After considering whatever financial difficulties led to the need for a reverse mortgage in the first place, if you are comfortable taking the loss and confident that your house is in order, feel free to take advantage of this option. But don't enter into the agreement if you will be stuck without additional options in case of later emergency.

- Obtaining renters, it almost goes without saying, is an effective method of reducing your mortgage obligation on a secondary property. If the market is soft, put some extra investment into searching for tenants both through print and internet advertising and among your family and friends. A decision to rent may require hard decisionmaking by you and your family; sometimes unresolved issues in relationships mean that a person's property is not being used to its full advantage. In any case, the time it takes to obtain counsel and work out issues is well worth the return. In some markets, rent is so high that the entire property could be purchased for cash for only four years' worth of rent (that shows you how much the time factor is valued by lenders). The question of renting out part or all of your primary property should be considered as well, especially if your primary property is not your final goal: finding a cheap intermediate place to hang your hat is sometimes worthwhile, as for individual owners or couples.

One of our friends rented out so many rooms of her house that she moved out into a livable trailer on the property! She still has full run of her house, but is making enough profit on it now that she can invest in maintaining a well-furnished trailer as well.

- Principal reduction offers can be made when you have other funds that can be applied to increasing your equity rather than their current purpose. Often homeowners hold a positive balance in another investment and a negative balance in debt owed that cancel each other out. If the investment has a significantly lesser likelihood of interest earnings than the likelihood of increase in housing prices, it's a good time to make a principal reduction offer, because investing in your own equity is then a better investment. This has been true, for instance, in 2008, when housing deflation was in check but stocks appeared to be in freefall. A savings account bearing insufficient interest is another potential resource for principal reduction.

Even if there is not a large difference in passive earnings, it's definitely wise to shift savings into equity if this can lead to paying off the mortgage by traditional means in as little as five to seven years. When the remaining term is that short, the cumulative loss of value attributed to interest is much less destructive to your capital, and the goal of finally slaying the mortgage beast is actually visible on the horizon. When the numbers are large enough, holding onto a savings account for a rainy day is not significantly better than holding onto an equity line of credit: the dollar bills you would receive from the bank are identical in each case and provide the same illusion of not being in debt in each case. (Debt freedom is not real until the mortgage dragon is slain, so holding a large savings balance is no help when it means resources are not being used for debt reduction.)

While principal reduction can be performed unilaterally by sending whatever small or large additions you like along with your mortgage payment, it is better to make an offer to the lender when dealing with significant amounts, to determine what type of refinance or modification can be offered in return. This process is usually uncomplicated. While this book is primarily about nonpayment, it's also true that -payment now- of any particular amount owed always means the perpetual right -not- to have to pay that amount -later- at any other time. On the other hand, on the traditional timetable, -not paying a mortgage amount now- means paying that amount later - two, three, or four times-, because of compounding interest. Paradoxically, using assets to pay debt today is one of the surest roads to the perpetual right of nonpayment, such as is enjoyed by those who have finally exterminated their mortgages!

The streamlined modification process

To review briefly, changing your loan without complex administrative processing can be done in several ways. But those of us with really difficult mortgages breathing down our necks need access to more formal methods. In the long run it is necessary, sooner or later, to satisfy the demands of these mutant Frankenstein monsters formally, in their own universes, the one in which their creators placed them. Those alternate universes are the reason that books like this are written, to guide us through the bankster's designated administrative labyrinths, mazes that rival those of any fictional mythos and that are limited only by modern imaginations.

The first such navigation method, because it's the most amicable and least likely to lead to bad blood later, is the loan modification process. Fannie Mae and Freddie Mac publish standard guidelines for loan modification processes, and lenders typically either state they follow the federal recommendations or publish their own amendments to the process. Under the federal process, over one million formal loan modifications have been successfully processed through 2011, and kinks have been ironed out in a streamlined process made easier in 2012, with less required paperwork.

The federal process requires the home to be your primary residence (not a speculative or investment property). Eligibility criteria are being underwater, paying over 38% of your budget to your mortgage, or being otherwise considered a high risk for lender loss. Though there are exceptions, many loan officers reject applications less than 90 days delinquent; but it doesn't hurt to test the waters by applying early if you have the time.

Requesting a loan modification amounts to telling the lenders that their best interests are served by "working out" or modifying the loan's terms, whether due to financial hardship or other factors affecting your contract. The new terms must be "better" for the lender, in particular by making it more likely for them to be repaid. The approval department will be looking for "risk mitigation," that is, evidence that they are probabilistically less likely to suffer loss under the new terms.

The loss mitigation department doesn't usually take the borrower's perspective that the best approach is to wait until the borrower repays, whenever that is. "Mitigation" might mean that your case is in the worst percentiles of risk and so it should be foreclosed as "unworkable" because foreclosing a small percentage of loans will theoretically save them time overall. "Mitigation" might mean that they don't trust you but looking at your numbers they think they can squeeze enough money out of you to make it worth their while. So be very cautious in all communication. Always present data recognizing the lender's perspective: don't think of your pitch in terms of how much you promise to pay but in terms of the percentage likelihood that your predictions will come true. Always present your data in the best light possible, and always think of your odds in the worst light possible.

Your first step is to contact the lender to determine whether they accept applications under the government loan modification program or whether they have their own internal process requirements. Get the physical address of the approval department. Then follow through as described below, making any adjustments for organizational idiosyncrasies.

Documentation

Keep in mind this caveat whenever compiling documents for the lender: anything you say "can and will" be used against you. While the documents have the purpose of demonstrating your financial picture to the lender for one process, you don't want them to become hostile witnesses in a different process like foreclosure. To protect against this risk, your financial picture need to demonstrate both that your current payment is exceedingly "unlivable" (speculative and risky to the lender), but that the requested change would make the fulfillment of the mortgage exceedingly "livable" (well-collateralized and safe to the lender). If your picture shows a high monthly amount of savings or (more often) of unnecessary expenses, you may not have the moral high ground to demand a change or, in fact, to avoid foreclosure, and the lender may tell you so. Aside from the general budget advice interspersed throughout this book, we'll have more to say about proper pictures that dissuade foreclosure later.

The application will consist of three basic forms and your backup documents. You (or else your detail-oriented best friend) really can handle the whole package without additional assistance. The rule of thumb used to be "the more the better," but under the streamlined process you can start with the three forms and then add what will complement the financial picture in your favor (e.g., hospital records in the event of medical hardship). These three forms are:

- Earnings verification, for the last two years. A month of paystubs from each workplace will work for many people, or audited financial statements if you work for yourself or have an accountant. Evidence of irregular earnings (such as via bank statements) should be supplemented by a narrative that supports an annual average. Tax forms are useful even if the federal definition of "income" is circuitously different from other accounting measures of income and can be misleading. Expenses are a backup form of earnings verification and are

important to demonstrate your need for lender mercy: bills of every kind including seasonal variations, especially unpaid bills or cutoff notices, flesh out this need with specifics. Inclusion of particular documents is at your discretion based on what target numbers you're seeking in your request for assistance (see below).
- Tax authorization. This is a simple statement (Internal Revenue Service form 4506T-EZ or a letter containing the same information) that authorizes the IRS to provide your lender with recent tax information. Very important: IRS authorization expires automatically, so when using this form with any process that may take a long time, find out the expiration date and make a calendar note to resend a new authorization if the process hasn't completed by then. Failure to reauthorize has, by itself, historically caused large proposed packages to be rejected by random nitpicky employees: don't take the risk of running into one of them with an expired form. The better your budget, the easier this step becomes.
- Request for mortgage assistance. This form is obtainable from the lender and describes your finances in standardized fashion. It attempts to convert a hardship letter (which sometimes can be and has been too melodramatic) into a cold, impersonal Q-and-A session that's easy on the lender's database.

Since eligibility hinges on the request form's data, tension exists between the need for accuracy and the desire for acceptability. Approval formulas are built from the banks' internal actuarial data to meet complex business requirements: your listed expenses, for instance, might be so many that the lender thinks you will never pay them back, or they might instead be so few that the lender's idea of a payment plan is way above the league you were playing in. The process positions you in the dubious, delicate balance of saying, "If only I get help then I can help myself." A lot of allegedly complex decisionmaking is simply reliance on the actuary department's decisions in creating very broad-based formulas that play upon these tensions. One of the known targets is that the federal process encourages mortgage expense to come out at 31% of total earnings, so keep that in mind when plugging the proposed rate changes into a spreadsheet amortization formula. Though lenders keep their approval formulas secret, various brokers have enough experience with the approvals to calculate proprietary algorithms that claim very high success rates at guessing the lender's approval methods.

If you want to enlist a real estate or legal professional who makes some form of eligibility guarantee or "how to get approved" claim, you'll probably get a specialist with this kind of experience: someone who shoots from the hip but is right good at it. You might need such a partner to analyze and "preapprove" your honest data, and you might want a creative accountant who can assist with budget categorizations that position your numbers in the best brackets. (Accountants are like snowflakes, since no two of them ever calculate the same bottom line from the same complex data: if you don't like the bottom line, ask again!) If success in any approval process is a very high priority, consider an expense for this kind of professional help.

When your request for assistance is complete, determine any supplemental documents desired by you or the servicer. A personalized hardship letter is important to establish your boundaries and your legal position: it expresses, in your own words, your plight to date, your goodwill attempt to remain domiciled and involved in your community on modified terms, and particular risks to you (i.e., threats to the lender's revenue stream) if the modification is not approved. If possible, document both your past inability to pay (e.g., bad old job) and your present ability to pay (e.g., good new job).

The hardest document to provide may be when Citi Mortgage or another bank requires you to make early calculation of the modified monthly payment, and the first month's payment enclosed as a trial of modification. Be prepared.

Definitely include in your package any correspondence to or from the lender that will help demonstrate your assertions, including sale attempts. Don't forget to copy the envelopes because of their postmark dates, as proof of receipt date is sometimes critical. After copying everything, send it to the lender's address for loan modification approvals, whatever the loss mitigation department is called; yes, you can spend a couple bucks to have it certified if you want proof you mailed it (or if the lender has a history of poor documentation).

Followup

Then keep after your lender by calling in every week or two. Employees are required to give you status updates that you can understand, even if the approval department may be insulated by not speaking to applicants directly. It's helpful to make a note of the time, date, employee, and result in each phone conversation: this is particularly important for noting promises and deadlines so that you can hold the lender to keeping their employee's word later. Don't be surprised if the application seems to bounce from one person to another: that's a symptom of the pressure on each employee to take -some- action within a departmental (30-day) deadline. Just close each conversation with a lender promise of the next action and deadline.

If the lender throws a hot potato back to you, be sure to answer immediately so as not to disrupt the process. Many demands for financial documents have only a 10-day window for response. Keep a copy of the postmark of any such answer you send.

When you finally get a response to your application, remember that you don't necessarily have to take the first offer rashly, especially if you are uncomfortable committing to the payment schedule. The modification may be temporary or require you to commit to higher payments later. You always have three options: in addition to taking the offer as is, you can negotiate to improve it, or abandon the process and work a different strategy (i.e., deed in lieu or short sale). Discuss the package deal with your intimates and be certain you won't be setting yourself up for failure or tempting the servicer to make a turnaround foreclosure.

The lender is taking risks too: they may be counting on receiving a federal incentive to assist them in closing your mod, so they have an incentive to hear a counteroffer. If you are dealing with a second mortgage, the lender has an extreme disincentive to foreclose, because foreclosure auctions almost never exceed the demands of the first mortgagor. The second mortgagor generally regards anything as better than nothing. The lender may therefore offer a trial modification period first, or may regard partial forbearance as a trial period. Compliance with the trial will be a factor in granting a longer-term modification, so the lender assumes you will not be exerting the right of nonpayment indefinitely: missing any payments may cause an immediate demand for any temporarily forgiven forbearance or trial reduction, plus attorney's and other fees, which can be a shock to the system.

Accordingly, don't run to apply for or accept a loan modification if there is real risk of failing a single trial payment. In this strategy the lender wants to know that your modified payment will not be too much different from your current anticipated payment. It works best when what you need is medium-term creative easing of the original demand that sounds middle-of-the-road when compared to the needs of millions of other homeowners: pleasing most of the people some of the time is the ultimate pragmatic goal of the federal program. So if you slip in the middle of the pack and do not make excessive demands, you benefit from the banks' miscalculations during the mortgage bubble and from federal administrators' desires to redistribute OPM (other people's money). On the other hand, if your need for the right of repudiation is deeper than what the feds have decided is a "reasonable" relaxation of mortgage demands, read the next chapters to find additional methods of nonpayment.

The fast track

When circumstances indicate that a loan modification process or other change will successfully seize money left on the table at this instant, dive in.

- The fastest way to go right in with an approachable lender is to retain a professional specializing in loan mods and prepare an application where every detail demands your modification be approved. Shepherding the process yourself has great benefits for self-education but does not always have the luxury of time: individualism can get it done quickly, but being walked through the process usually gets it done more quickly. Seek someone who can keep you posted immediately on any lender communications, especially those that require 10-day or 30-day responses. The trust factor is essential.

The lenders are "approachable" if evidence shows they have some money left on the table. You can use advertisements to gauge rates and amortizations to see if you're getting a fair shake or if you're ripe for refinance. You can easily calculate your ratio of mortgage to earnings: if it's over 38%, you're likely to be as eligible for a modification as anyone. The older your mortgage, the greater your equity and the more likely your acceptance.

Since loan modifications have a wide variance in approval times and the federal program is designed to be applied for by literally anyone, no professional has an inside-track advantage over the do-it-yourself steps in this chapter. What professionals do have, however, is experience that gives them a high likelihood in getting an application right the first time. When the loan modification is your best strategy and speed is essential, consider delegating.

The other strategies for adjusting your loan obligations can generally be accomplished quickly when the right conditions exist:

- Principal reduction can be performed unilaterally anytime you can convert assets. It provides an immediate stress relief.
- Refinance can be smooth if advertised rates are much lower than your current rates.
- Forbearance can be very quickly approved if requested to suspend collections during a modification or short-sale package.
- If private mortgage insurance exists on the property, it can provide temporary relief.
- If you're over 62 or otherwise qualify, arrange for a reverse mortgage to take advantage of the equity you already own.
- If you can find a renter quickly among your social network, or the market is good, jump in. Do the math on comparables.

The delay track

Even if none of the various modifications gives you an immediate clear advantage, they can still be used to hold your position as part of a long-term multiphase approach. Delay is all about asking the lender to wait for a reasonably pending event (a good-faith modification application, even if unlikely; engagement of a renter; reaching age 62; final negotiations on principal reduction; etc.).

- If your first application for loan modification is denied, you have the right to keep making offers. Backing up, getting a fresh pair of eyes on the situation, and making a different application that takes the intervening months into account may make the second application more successful at achieving your ultimate goals. Further consultation with professionals may help prepare a second offer that also considers the lender's stated repositioning upon rejecting the first offer. Changes in either earnings or expenses can be regarded as reasonable cause for reapplying, and such lifestyle changes are often not difficult to make, even artificially. While the lender will not regard successive applications as an excuse for back-to-back episodes of total nonpayment, demonstration of either goodwill or of treading water (keeping the delinquency period constant) will be favorable to the later applications.
- As an alternate delay, instead of following up immediately with a successive application, you can express a desire to rent or short-sell your property. You may or may not want to inform the lender. Proof that you are advertising your location for sale or rent and working with a Realtor does have value in suggesting that the lender might see the money you're angling to obtain. If you obtain a renter, decided what to do with the extra cash.
- If you're just under 62, write an initial hardship letter now and wait out the time it takes to set up a reverse mortgage. Requesting a loan modification in the interim won't hurt at all.
- While it provides an immediate relief from further destructive interest, a principal reduction offer can also be

used as one means of delay. If you have other assets that you are comfortable shifting into real estate equity, you can cash the assets to pay down part of your mortgage on the condition that you obtain a loan modification that recognizes the paydown. This will lower your payments for the short term, or for the life of the mortgage, to give you time to act on or research one of the other strategies.

Chapter 6

Stand Your Ground

While the loan modification process takes advantage of "loose" bank and government money to obtain forgiveness of principal and abatement of interest, the short sale process is a scrupulous use of other people's money to leverage the bank's more tightly held money to the same purpose. By definition, a "short" sale means the property is already underwater, so even though a buyer stands as collateral, that collateral doesn't completely satisfy the current mortgage. The lender would receive the proceeds, but is forced by the imminence of the market transaction to forgive the remainder of the debt (or, when the difference is serious, to convert some or all of it to a promissory note that is much easier for you to pay off than the mortgage). In many states (though not large markets like Florida) the law requires the difference to be forgiven in all short sales.

It works like this. First, you suspend your natural desire to get back what you paid, or even what you owe: you reconcile yourself to getting part of what you owe covered by the buyer's money, and part of it covered by the lender's deficiency waiver, and possibly paying out a remaining part of it separately as a loss (we hope you invested your squatter rent). You then advertise like crazy in the ordinary third-party real estate market. Since you've abandoned the high hopes and are offering an at-market or easily below-market price, prospective buyers are not as hard to find as you might think. Since you explain that it's a short sale and requires your lender to approve it, the buyer has the advantage of not needing to make a commitment immediately: the buyer's final decision can be postponed until the lender's decision, which usually takes at least two months. Because the buyer needs to make an initial good-faith offer but does not need a final decision until later, it's very possible to sell the property to a close relative or associate (a white knight) who can be trusted to work with you during the short sale process; your social circle should be told of your plans just as much as the strangers you advertise to.

The buyer offer may be the hardest piece of the puzzle to find so the search needs to begin as soon as you know you're pursuing a short sale. If you make the decision to sell today, begin listing the property today if possible. Using a real estate agent is fine, but don't neglect the by-owner advertising and word of mouth that successfully closes a sizable plurality of all real estate sales.

Combined, the package process and the monitoring of potential buyers are more labor-intensive than other options. If you believe short sale is the best strategy and you steel yourself to see it through to completion, the additional documentation and followup tasks should not cause a major problem. Since this is the only option that combines strong financial skills with strong sales skills, a well-rounded person should be able to complete it, as well as a person who knows how to delegate the tough parts to another personality type. Because of the potential deficiency waiver, the labor is well worth your while. There will also be sales expenses, so don't neglect to account for these in calculating the final price allocation.

Since it is necessary to obtain the lender's final approval on a short sale, which can be withheld, start the process of working with the lender (not against) by mentioning the intent to short-sell in your hardship letter. The hardship needs to be new (not preexisting), but it need not be shown to be temporary (as it would in a loan modification). If you know you want to start with a short sale, announce the intent to stop paying in the hardship letter (or, if you've already begun nonpayment, formally state the date you consider it to have begun); believe it or not, your being delinquent (usually at least 3 months) is a factor in favor of approving the short sale. Any cosigners on the mortgage should also demonstrate inability or disinclination to pay in the hardship letter. The other lender condition is that, while your price can be ridiculously low, you -don't- want it to be lower than what the lender thinks it can get in a foreclosure auction. Make sure you've interviewed the loss mitigator to discuss these points before mailing the initial hardship letter.

Incidentally, if you're -not- underwater, you also have the option of carrying out a traditional sale without restrictions. Most of the advice in this chapter applies in that case as well. But if staying in your home is an important part of your plan, traditional sale may not be indicated.

If you decide you'll need professional help with a sale, many short-sale specialists recognize that their fees will be deferred until the sale completes. Take advantage of this arrangement. Be sure you know what services the professional is and is not offering.

The short sale package

The lender should have a checklist of documentation required for its process. Start by gathering documentation of earnings and expense verification and supplemental documents described in chapter 5 for the loan modification process: pay statements, bank statements, tax and mortgage payments, etc. Banks may also require an audited financial statement, as well as your identification card or driver's license. In a short sale, it is typical to include the realty's property information sheet, along with appraisal and floorplan data.

Definitely include a copy of your initial hardship letter, or rewrite and reprint parts of it to accommodate any changed situation. Since a short sale does not have its own request form for mortgage assistance, the hardship letter should summarize the earnings and expense numbers and emphasize the current leftover funds (or shortfall) after "necessary" expenses are paid. (An account can pack a lot of meaning into that word "necessary," if necessary.) The facts disclosed in this letter will be a guideline for the lender to work from. As always, the letter's purpose is to make the case that your proposed alternative (short sale) is better for the lender than a unilateral foreclosure: this is done both by affirming the likelihood of the lender getting paid rapidly and sufficiently and by alluding indirectly to the risks that a foreclosure would not be a neat and tidy affair. (One hint for the lender is your commanding and proactive tone in adversity, which suggests the same in a hypothetical foreclosure. Another hint is if you demonstrate that the likely short sale price is much higher than comparable distressed auction prices: "distressed auction" is a codeword indicating foreclosure.)

Your package is completed when you have a signed offer from a qualified buyer. Some states require this to be in the form of a purchase agreement with a rider explaining the short-sale contingency: each state has a standard real estate contract that can be found online that will guide you in documenting the offer. Again, the buyer should be prepared to prove a funding source (cash or the ability to earn a mortgage payment) and to follow through if approved.

In a state where deficiency waivers are not automatic, the lender may require a deficiency judgment as part of the package, requiring you to pay down a set promissory note value over the coming years or decades: this allows you (and to some degree the buyer) the right to decline the acceptance offer if it's an unsuitable repayment plan for you. This means the buyer is not necessarily locked in: the closer you are with the buyer, the better you can work out a mutually beneficial plan.

The buyer can generally be found by the traditional routes. You can list the property with a real estate agent or by owner. Either way you'll want to have ready summaries of the sale opportunity via boilerplate flyers or emails with good photos. Disseminate your ads by word of mouth and personal handoff; by community bulletin boards; by targeted direct mail or email; by online listings and social media (both local and in other regions where snowbirds and other multiproperty owners might be found); by enlisting friends in family in the search; and by every other means. If you're in the majority, a sales personality does not come naturally; in this case you can either decide to cultivate an adaptive sales-oriented personality, or to ask one of your more talkative friends (someone to whom the talent usually does come naturally).

At any rate, don't neglect the work involved in marketing your own property: because of its distinct benefits, a short sale really is worth the extra time. Short sales allow you to stay in your home on your terms and frequently stop foreclosures and other negatives cold. They offer low credit risk and smoother transition to credit situations after the sale. The search for a well-heeled buyer to take on an as-is property (including automatic resolution of delinquent taxes and association fees) appeals naturally to professional assistants, who are willing to wait to be paid until they can successfully help you by scaring up the funding. And because debt forgiveness is so often part of the package, the mechanism of finding a sufficient amount of other people's money to leverage an equally large amount of the lender's money into the deal is financially one of the best alternatives available. Always consider both the additional time, labor, and expense in tandem with the potential benefits in debt release (ultimately fungible to repay you for your time and labor) when making your decision.

The approval process

It's true, lots can go wrong during approval, but it can usually be fixed either immediately or in the next round of the process.

- As with loan modifications, call the lender frequently for status conferences. You will be assigned a negotiator for these discussions. In the most basic terms, every stage allows the lender another month to consider its decision (e.g., ordering an appraisal or opinion, submitting the file from negotiations to review, producing the final decision letter, and any personnel changes along the way). Keeping your hand held through this portion of the labyrinth is entirely the lender's responsibility, but only if you keep pestering. To them, no news is good news and silence means consent. Don't stay silent if you want them to move.
- Respond rapidly to any requests for additional documents, including another rewritten hardship letter if its text needs adjusting. A good filing system, or a professional assistant, can help fulfill these requests on time. At the same time, keep listening for opportunities to make your own requests for information. If a negotiator seems willing or desirous to guide you verbally or indirectly to make a certain conclusion or categorization, such cues are usually given more in your interests than as fishing expeditions for adverse evidence. Sometimes the lender will hint at needing to reach a particular range of numbers, whether it's your expenses, your proposed sales price, or your ratio of mortgage to earnings:

play along and get an accounting that's close to that number whenever possible. They're called negotiators for a reason.
- Keep your buyer in the loop about once a month, or when you have news from the lender. Stay intimate with your buyer and keep praising their patience with a lender process that has little outside accountability. Remind them (as you remind yourself) not to worry about the time factor, as an approval will always happen sooner or later given enough persistence in cycling the process.
- Be patient if your negotiator, or your buyer, bails out on you due to time commitments. There's always time to find another one. (If your situation is so grave that even nonpayment doesn't keep the wolf from the door, you should be reading more books than this one.)
 Just as you shouldn't be surprised by curveballs, on the other hand, you shouldn't be surprised if everything goes right the first time.
- When the lender finally approves your sale, you are on the standard real estate closing track. You can negotiate your closing date up to about three or even four months out, and prepare to move out (or rent back the property you are selling). The lender will assign you a closing agent and the process is noncontroversial from there.
- As described, deficiency waivers on short sales are automatic in some states. Further, via the Mortgage Forgiveness Debt Relief Act of 2007, deficiency waivers are also automatic on primary properties through 2012 (and there is hope that this provision will not sunset the next year either). But keep in mind: to the degree that your deficiency is not waived, you will be asked to pay back no-interest promissory notes for however many years it takes to retire them; and to the degree that your deficiency is waived, you should receive IRS Form 1099-C reporting the degree to which the waived (forgiven) debt is regarded as income and tax liability. So there's a hit either way. If the deficiency waiver is partial, you make the payback first, and you have the appropriate tax consequences of debt forgiveness deferred until the payback is complete, but you don't generally escape either of them.

- While a short sale does affect your credit rating, you can still recover from it quickly: one study shows an average drop in FICO scores of less than 100 points for short sales and deeds in lieu (due to the debt forgiveness factor), compared to around 300 points for foreclosures. However, we've also known specialists to game the numbers in either direction, so these are estimates, and it's possible an experienced foreclosure or bankruptcy attorney can minimize your credit loss in these extremities. Even so, the credentialing deficit of a short sale can usually be rebuilt within about two years, or less if you work with a credit monitoring and repair service, while the foreclosure or bankruptcy will be remembered for up to seven years.

The fast track

A chief advantage of compiling a short sale package quickly is that it throws the ball at the lender, because the package can be written in 1-2 weeks but it takes 2-6 months to process. This gives you the momentum and the nonpayment rights and puts the onus of decisionmaking on the lender. Plus, if you know someone who can serve as a prospective qualified buyer at an "extreme undercut" price, there is little risk in convincing that person to make a written offer with financials, and there is greatly leveraged potential if the lender forgives some of your debt as part of the package. The buyer might also be convinced to let you continue to live in the property under a rental agreement, which means that the buyer not only takes possession for a low price but also gets the benefit of your rent payments to assist in covering the buyer's mortgage.

- Beginning with word of mouth sometimes leads to a rapid short sale package. If you have a family member, close friend, or trustworthy acquaintance who can be persuaded to take on the property for a greatly reduced price, especially to keep the property within your family or network of friends, it's worth making the offer. As long as the proposed buyer can demonstrate the proven ability to pay the low price either in cash or over time, the package can be presented in good faith: even though the price is ridiculously low, the buyer and seller agree on it (which makes it a market valuation) and the only question for the lenders is how much debt they want to forgive. You and the prospective buyer should agree on whether you intend to move out or stay and rent, if the sale should close.

Even if you suspect the lender will reject the plan out of hand, you can begin the nonpayment window immediately upon the decision to seek out a prospective buyer. If you get a rejection you can shift to the delay track and continue to prosecute your short sale with the market research you've done in the interim. If you get a surprise acceptance at a low rate and are asked to cover all or part of a deficiency, you and the buyer still have the option to back out if you believe there is not enough debt forgiveness involved. In the rare event that you get a complete deficiency waiver on a rock-bottom price, I would think you'd take it! That kind of debt forgiveness doesn't come often, and you can either stay at home by renting from the new owner, or move out to a new location (you have the right to negotiate the closing date and thus how much time you need to move out).

- In a healthy real estate market, work out the value based on local comparables that will be comfortable to you even if you have to pay the difference between your sale price and the current debt. If your immediate social circle doesn't contain a white knight, get your advertising going on all fronts, starting with a price suitable for the market's valuation. Then write a short sale package on your first offer and throw the ball unexpectedly into the lender's court. For lenders to process and make final decisions on short sale packages takes two to six months anyway, but as long as you're listing and not paying the mortgage, you have the luxury of that "squatter rent" over the months that each lender processing event takes.
- In a soft real estate market, take the same approach but start with a ridiculously low offer that you can live with if the worst case arises. This allows you to submit your first short sale package quickly even if the offer is so low it's likely to be rejected, and it gets the jump on your lender.

The delay track

If you began the short sale process by sending a hardship letter, you have covered your bases even when a soft market means your property is not expected to move quickly. In this case you can easily hold off your creditor indefinitely by giving a monthly report evidencing your "due diligence." This means documentation proving that you have made a reasonable number of contact attempts, advertisements, inquiry followups, showings, and other seller activity. As long as you show this every month, the lender has no right to complain and would be premature to foreclose.

- If you're confident the house will sell eventually, inform the lender in your hardship letter that the property has been listed for short sale. Then reduce risk of foreclosing action by keeping regular contact with the lender even if you don't have a buyer and a completed application package.
- If you're not confident the house will sell in a reasonable period, begin the short sale package anyway, but discuss a deed in lieu with the lender on the same timeline. If you and the lender set a deadline and don't find a buyer, the lender will have been warmed up to the deed-in-lieu process.
- If you're not known to be in immediate jeopardy of foreclosure but part of your problem is that you've recently had an embarrassing increase in expenses (whether this is by accident or via flareup of bad habits), there is a very strategic delay move for those who can regain self-control. Prepare the bulk of your short sale documents but do not present them to the lender for several months; you might even engage in a different strategy first (refinance, rental, modification) and mention that in your initial hardship letter rather than the short sale. The reason for this delay is that, for the next six months, you plan to go on an essentials-only spending diet and to rebuild your savings (don't forget squatter rent). Most level-headed people can commit to short-term lifestyle changes that have significant long-term benefit, and this is one of those. Keep your receipts for these six months and -then- submit the short-sale package. Instead of profligacy the lender will see a self-disciplined, consistent, reasonable

spending record that also conveniently demonstrates a lack of ability to afford the current mortgage. The lenders won't hold your savings against you (they may expect to obtain your savings themselves as part of the package), but they -will- hold an irresponsible spending record against you, as it suggests you are a low-hanging fruit in the foreclosure process. Curb the bad habits, and only give yourself a responsible splurge after you close the sale.

- Another option when you have a potential white knight is to prepare a short sale package in advance as a protective measure against foreclosure, but not to send it. This can be done if you suspect risk of foreclosure for other reasons, and can occur even while the property is listed for short sale to an alternate buyer, or while the property is in a loan modification or other process. What happens is that, when your lender files for foreclosure with the courts, you can submit the short sale package to suspend or delay the foreclosure. While this requires more than usual cooperation from the buyer, it is often possible to achieve with acquaintances or motivated buyers. Remember that the buyer is likely to receive the property at a reduced price by partaking in the lender's forgiveness, so the buyer might well be persuaded to hold off on submitting the sale if the foreclosure is expected soon.
- Finally, if the short sale seems to be falling apart because of disagreement about the deficiency waiver in a state that allows it, see chapter 8 for a method of salvaging the deal by shifting to a naked deed in lieu. Most difficulties about deficiency waivers can be understood by reviewing that chapter and regrouping one's plan to compensate for the lender's position.

Chapter 7

Call the Shots (I)

The deed in lieu of foreclosure is exactly what it sounds like, a direct and often sudden offer to the lender to preempt their risk by letting them have the house back. Like the short sale, its benefits are that it keeps you in your home while the lender is considering it and also for some time after if successful; that it releases all or most of your liability; that it minimizes credit damage compared to foreclosure (credit repair usually takes only two years); and that it can also be used to delay a day of reckoning as part of a longer strategy. But by the time you're considering a deed in lieu, it usually means your other options have not panned out, because a deed in lieu is practically equivalent to asking the lender to accept a short sale but with itself as buyer. If there is no advantage to having a third-party buyer via short sale, then deed in lieu should be weighed with equal consideration.

The lender has no obligation to waive the deficiency, so, to offer a deed in lieu, always speak assumptively as if getting a deficiency waiver is a foregone conclusion; this presumption can be first stated in your hardship letter or by writing "no deficiency" on the application. If you leave it unstated, the lender may beat you to the punch by assuming contrarily that you will pay a large deficiency. After discussing deeds in lieu generally in this chapter, we will go into the variations of handling deficiencies in chapter 8. Again, the numerical goal in either case is to find out through hard negotiation what the lender expects through foreclosure, and to demonstrate that a deed offering and an undistressed sale will generate a -higher- return for the lender. The secondary logistical goal is to convince the lender that a cooperative deed in lieu will allow the lender to sell the property -faster- than a foreclosure with an uncooperative homeowner (you) who knows how to suspend, block, and redirect foreclosure actions, and to defeat them outright if the lender should be found to have made a single miscalculation.

You will probably want at least to test the waters with refinance, modification, or sale first to eliminate them as alternatives. Also in common with the short sale, a deed in lieu usually assumes an extended hardship and a longer period of nonpayment (delinquency).

The first variation of deed in lieu for you to investigate is a deed for lease. "Deed-For-Lease" is a trademark of Fannie Mae, so we will describe the process as if they are the lender. (If your investigation shows the official noteholder is some other lender, always ask if they offer a similar leaseback program in connection with your offering a deed in lieu. Many good leasing options are known.) If a Deed-For-Lease succeeds, you will be transferring your home to Fannie Mae with the guarantee that you can lease it back from them at a new area-comparable rate for an extendible period starting with a year. Not only will you be staying in your home indefinitely without the initial deposit that a renter usually pays, but you will also have escaped the bulk of your liability. Fannie Mae also offers relocation assistance as an alternative to extending the lease.

This process does not typically require as much paperwork as a modification or short sale. After submitting an initial application obtainable from your mortgage company, along with earnings and expense verification and a hardship letter, you will be assigned a property manager and an inspection will be ordered. Your patience while the manager reviews your submissions and gets additional information will be expected. If you qualify, you will be presented a deed in lieu and a lease agreement together for your signature, and the lender will have a statutory period to finalize acceptance. After the closing date your first-year lease begins and rent is paid monthly to the property manager.

If instead you are likely to be ready to leave your home soon, you can offer the deed in lieu without the lease option. Either way you are directing the process away from foreclosure rather than waiting for the process to direct itself in the other direction.

If the full deficiency waiver succeeds, remember that the lender typically tells the IRS about the amount of debt forgiveness.

To determine the likelihood of your offer succeeding, calculate the comparable property value and the comparable distressed auction value, and estimate the amount that the lender would be required to waive (the difference between your debt and the comparable property value). If the waiver is small enough, proceed assumptively as if the waiver is an essential element of the package. Then work your negotiator like a fellow negotiator. Don't take for granted any statement about the negotiator not having leeway to modify proposals: the negotiator will always hear another offer and may "check with a supervisor," and the haggling skills you may have learned at the pawn shop will repay you handsomely.

The fast track

The deed in lieu is most effective when the lender has verbally or indirectly expressed a fear of the risks of foreclosure. If the subject of foreclosure comes up, you have an opportunity to probe your contact to find out who is making the decision and what considerations will be used. We presume you have already evidenced that the lender's risks in foreclosure are severe, starting indirectly with your hardship letter, and continuing via more direct demonstrations (to be inferred through your writing style) that you have the power and knowledge to tie up or even defeat a foreclosure action by virtue of superior argumentation, application of law, and persistence.

- If foreclosure is a risk, submit a deed-for-lease package immediately to tie up the lender with an evaluation decision. Emphasize in writing that such a package is much better for the lender than a drawn-out foreclosure process. Emphasize that you are prepared to fight foreclosure and make it more costly than it is worth to the lender. Simply stating your preparations can be perceived as a sufficient threat to keep the lender favoring your offering.
Calculate the comparable property value and the comparable distressed auction value, and estimate the amount that the lender would be required to waive (the difference between your debt and the comparable property value). If the waiver

is small enough, proceed assumptively as if the waiver is an essential element of the package.
- If you are considering leaving your home, submit the package as a standard deed in lieu with deficiency waiver, without the lease option.
- If your initial offering does not succeed, use it as a springboard to continue negotiating until you have a handle on what the negotiator really wants and you can switch to the naked deed in lieu or another strategy.

he delay track

By making a good-faith offering, even if you extend it over a series of negotiations, you take advantage of other lender fears. No lender wants to get vetoed by another mortgagor or lienholder. No lender wants to get stuck with vacant property at severe risk of vandalism or metal theft. What the lender's employees want is to get your particular case off their desks and into an acceptable category. Deed in lieu is the fallback category that can be prosecuted and reoffered as long as the lender is still talking to you.

- If deed in lieu seems indicated but time is your greatest need, the process is similar, but move more slowly. First, keep in contact with the lender once or twice a month, but only make commitments to your strategies if there is a genuine threat or if the negotiator gives a nonverbal cue of new disinterest that signals contemplation of a change in your status. Every month or two make another step demonstrating that you are making genuine offers that are not complete because of a logistical step on their or your part, or that you intend to and are prepared to employ a strategy but it is not actionable yet (e.g., a short sale). Have the deed-in-lieu paperwork ready so it can be submitted in a pinch, and while that offer is being processed prepare a second one in case it needs submission immediately after rejection of the first.
- If you have a second mortgage, play one against the other. The first mortgagor will be more willing to accept a deed in lieu (or short sale or other package), so you emphasize that

acceptingness in responding to the second mortgagor's threats. The second mortgagor will be more willing to negotiate a partial paydown, because their need for immediate resolution and their risk of loss via bankruptcy is greater, so you save some of your resources for them, and emphasize your need for second-mortgage leeway in playing up a deficiency waiver with the first mortgagor. While this careful balance often looks intractable due to the curious love-triangle problem inherent in a second mortgage, it can still be worked to your favor. Keep negotiating even in the face of absolute refusals; you could always be reassigned to other staff. All the same, be prepared to move to naked deed in lieu, bankruptcy threats, foreclosure defenses, or other tactics described herein if you genuinely lose hope in prosecuting a deed in lieu with deficiency waiver.
- All this time, continue to build a relationship with your lender's staff that is fraternal rather than adversarial. Convince them you really do share their interests in getting the value permitted by law for their contract; emphasize whether your holding out is due to not knowing how to get them that value (can't pay), or due to polite, amicable disagreement about what that value is (won't pay). Even when you are working adverse possession or nonpayment, you can still approach the lender with a straight face, because they deal with others doing the same on a regular basis, and they will respect your forthrightness more than the shiftiness of the bait-and-switch operators they often meet.

The benefits of collegiality are that they take advantage of the lender's secret fears of vandalism and theft. While lenders have a writeoff category for damage to property they control, they want as little exposure to this risk as possible. This is a solid argument that a deed for lease, to you of all people, is far better than foreclosing, forcing bankruptcy, or even a deed in lieu with an eviction. Since most everyone at this point has faced severe neighborhood property devaluation, it should be easy to bring up examples of local vandalism and theft, as well as to refer to ordinary depreciation through wear and tear (whether real or projected). Playing upon these risks while continuing to stand as a good-faith advocate of a deed in lieu will slant the odds in your favor.

Chapter 8

Call the Shots (II)

Usually, a deed in lieu -without- a deficiency waiver represents a shift from the first deed-in-lieu offer. This shift allows you to use your promise to pay the deficiency later (i.e., not to waive it) as a bargaining chip in a later round.

A second path in is if a short sale failed because the lender refused to waive deficiency: sometimes that indicates the negotiator is ready to move directly to a naked deed in lieu. The tactical move is similar to the shift from on original deed-in-lieu offer.

Do -not- jump right to a naked deed in lieu simply because a professional recommends it, because such a recommendation is usually in their interests, not yours. Instead, build to such a proposal from one of the other strategies.

In either of the first two cases, watch for the point in negotiations that the short sale or deed in lieu seems to reach a bottleneck because the amount the proposed new property owner is offering to pay, plus the amount the lender is offering to forgive, don't yet reach the total amount owed. The lender's debt forgiveness amount is closely tied to its beliefs about resale prices in an auction of their real estate owned due to either foreclosure or deed in lieu.

Call their bluff on this belief. It amounts to an unstated claim that they can get more for selling it than you have been able to get. Turn the tables by offering the deed in lieu with only a partial deficiency waiver or none at all. It's as if you're suddenly offering to help them sell it at the price they want rather than insisting on doing it yourself for a lower return. At the point where your negotiator is talking about hard numbers and tipping his or her hand by hinting about their actuarial target, you seize the late-game opportunity you've been patiently waiting for and offering to meet that target in your next deed-in-lieu offer.

We know a Miami couple who had just reached the right negotiation point; they had gotten a short sale approval and had an immediate decision to make on an inadequate partial deficiency waiver. They wanted to know about applying for a deed in lieu and turned to a local attorney. The lawyer directed them to modifying and reattempting the short sale instead of going for the jugular by seizing upon the lender's exposed insistence that there was more money to be gained from the property. This couple didn't get the timely advice they needed, and it was a missed opportunity for the attorney and a lesson learned all around.

The reason this move works is that it's a win-win. If the lender wasn't bluffing and they really believe they can get their target number by owning the property themselves, they will usually be persuaded to accept a deed in lieu rather than foreclosure, especially if your hardship letter indicated you're still a good risk for lease rather than mortgage. On the other hand, if their bluff is called when you ask them their targets outright, their retreat on this point allows you the judo move of reproposing the prior negotiation in a strengthened light, i.e., the knowledge that your proposed short sale or deficiency waiver is by all evidence the best game going. (The only negotiator this doesn't work on is the self-guarded type who never tips a hand: if you recognize that you're facing this type of person, the lender may have already decided on eventual foreclosure regardless of their admissions of the reasonability of alternatives, they may have assigned you a hardcase as a means of clearing out their deadwood, and you and your supports should prepare for the worst.)

Make sure you've understood the basics of the process described in the previous chapter. In particular, since some or all of the debt will not be forgiven, you will be required to make a repayment agreement: you might succeed in getting a repayment plan as peachy as one with a short sale, but be prepared to counteroffer if you don't. The portion forgiven is expected to be tax reported via Form 1099-C, to which you respond by ensuring your tax preparer has read the applicable tax laws and given you the best advice.

If you're in such trouble that all repayment plans are intractable, keep in the delay track, keep your eyes open for signals to shift strategy, but, most important, keep your heart and soul committed to escaping the trap laid for you when you were tricked into a mortgage that would go sour later. Improbable as the story goes, I can't help but think of David Niven portraying Phileas Fogg traveling around the world in 80 days in order to win a wager. After spending myriads of pounds, and even purchasing the ship he stood on so that its cargo and riggings could be burned up to increase its speed, he finally stood disconsolate at the furnace and, in a sudden decision, threw in his own umbrella and hat. This kind of dedication ultimately pays off, as Jules Verne demonstrated, and as we hope your own real-life story will also flesh out. In the vagaries of time and chance, sooner or later a lifeline always appears.

Bankruptcy and other unilaterals

- To declare bankruptcy is to ask for all-round amnesty to give you the privilege of leaping forward from some arbitrary negative credit number, to zero. Unlike all the main strategies in this book, its appeal for free money (i.e., credit) is based on charity rather than on right, and on your inability rather than your resourcefulness. While bankruptcy is useful for restructuring, especially under expert guidance with experience in credit consequences and de novo budgeting, we do not give it much space because it doesn't keep you in your home and doesn't actually protect your right of nonpayment. Instead, everything you own is divided among the creditors, anything that can be attached to you after the bankruptcy pursues you with a vengeance (enforced unofficially but ubiquitously by your destroyed credit), and your claims of adverse possession and lender failure are washed away by eviction and inability to prosecute.
  It is appropriate to consider bankruptcy in the worst cases and expert counseling is available; it is even appropriate to use the risk of your eventual decision to take Chapter 7 as a bargaining chip. We are hopeful, however, that this book has provided you enough alternatives that you never need to take that step.

- "Jingle mail" is another unilateral move. This includes any decision to walk away from a property and wash one's hands, whether or not you actually mail the keys back to the lender. This too may have a moral backing but totally destroys the right of adverse possession and of satisfaction of lender disinterest. Again, given the alternatives, we believe jingle mail is for speculators and that staying the course, without invoking the extra logistics of moving from your primary home, is always worth the effort of focusing on your true goals.
- Urban squatting, while we're on the subject, is also an increasingly popular "Occupy" strategy that has been defended with high-road arguments. When you are facing the risk of moving out due to a short sale or deed in lieu, you may be tempted to become a squatter. If you have a preexisting tie to a property that gives you a colorable right of temporary occupation, and if you can use temporary occupation to put in sweat equity to work to demonstrate to the owner that your presence improves the property on a continuous basis, this position could be understood. But we are conscious that the majority of behavior defended as "urban squatting" does not occur on legally defensible grounds but on emotional invocations of higher justice, and we remind readers that higher justice always deigns to work through existing lower authorities and courts, even if statutory and case law contains temporary errors. Civil disobedience is a long-cherished right that remains right by remaining civil. While most of our strategies will keep you domiciled indefinitely, if you're ready to move we are hopeful that we've presented enough options that give you a workable transition window so that your presence will be regarded under much better terms than "squatting."

The fast track

Returning to the subject, the primary benefit of a naked deed in lieu is that it avoids outright foreclosure and its credit damage, as well as lender risks, by settling quickly.

- If you know upfront that you'll be comfortable paying the deficiency in a loan note over time, and you have an alternative place to go, it's possible to offer a naked deed in lieu as your first string. This is not true of many, so this offering usually appears later in the strategy pool. But, when you know your hardship is temporary and you have the resources to back out of your mortgage this way (such as a trust or retirement fund), your ability to offer the deed in lieu without deficiency waiver will be respected.
- As described, when a short sale or deficiency waiver is causing a holdup and it's clear the negotiator is angling for something else, use the judo move of jumping right to the naked deed in lieu. The negotiator will either join you on the new track or be forced to reconsider the old track more helpfully.

The delay track

A deed in lieu without deficiency waiver may be preferable if you need to absorb or deal with secondary liens or mortgages. As stated, the second mortgage runs the risk of zero return, or a mere pittance, in a foreclosure or bankruptcy action: so they are anxious to count the credit they extended either as receivable or as justified writedown. That makes them less likely to accept an offer unless part of their deficiency is not waived and the repayment plan is reasonable.

- First, play out the deed in lieu with deficiency waiver as long as possible. Make the package work for the first mortgage. If you get an outright rejection on behalf of the second mortgage, offer partial or full payment of the deficiency. This becomes a naked deed in lieu as a bargaining chip at that point. Follow through on the delay steps mentioned in the previous chapter. Because the only difference after removing the waiver is that you will probably have a note after the deed in lieu, requiring you to make a small monthly payment to satisfy the difference in addition to whatever new living expenses you have, the math can still work out given the right adjustments.

- Sometimes one must accept that the deed in lieu is only a delay but not a prevention of a foreclosure. In a case in South Carolina, a homeowner offered a naked deed in lieu as an alternative after being foreclosed on. This "proactivity" happened rather late, after almost $1 million in home value had already been lost from the notional price and the homeowner had already run out of resources, including retirement funds. This was a good interim step and removed the risk of foreclosing the first mortgage, which would ordinarily be sufficient, but there was a second mortgagor who exerted veto power by holding out for $100,000 to be satisfied on a line of credit. A holdout due to a second mortgage is a real problem and that lender has every right to be enfolded in the final solution.

In this case the homeowner had volunteered the information that bankruptcy would be almost unthinkable because of professional reputation, and had also kept payments relatively current instead of saving them in a squatter escrow account, both of which gave the second mortgagor an unnecessary edge. The homeowner needed to be able to take the risk of bankruptcy or first-mortgage foreclosure to the brink if necessary, to emphasize the risk that the second mortgage would receive zero in the settlement, and this threat did not happen. Instead, while the second mortgagor did not have resale potential, they were apparently hoping either to recoup the funds via a judgment against someone who still remained a sufficiently good credit risk, or they were hoping to have a formal writeoff as "allowable" bad-debt loss.

Negotiating the demanded number down did not go far or have any prospects of reaching immediate ability to satisfy a note (only about $20,000 could be freed up for this purpose anyway). In the end, the homeowner has been left with the foreclosure defense options described in the next chapter, and with the possibility that a short sale might still arise or that a reverse mortgage qualification might be worked out in a couple years. The cashflow decisions required for safe conveyance to that point, including scuttling one's credit rating, have not been easy and the situation has remained ongoing.

- When all else fails, remember your undivided dedication to the ideal, such as that portrayed in the incorrigible character Phileas Fogg. Wake up every day committing to find the solution; literally, try everything; divide your time seven different ways if necessary. Every transition means that you're going somewhere, and, wherever you go, there you are. If you've pursued the strategies in this book, and continue to pursue them even if foreclosed upon, this country and this world are such that you will find a way to rekindle your American dream sooner or later. Never give up.

Chapter 9

Frustrate Foreclosers

The disappointing and yet invigorating challenge of being foreclosed on is not a picnic, but it's not a prison sentence either. Remember that you hold the keys, not the lenders, as we'll reaffirm before the end of this book. In yet another paradox, we know numerous homeowners who have left foreclosure proceedings better off than when they came in. Rely on your support network to offload the emotional trauma you'll be likely to face, especially if your circle has grown since you first took responsibility to escape the mortgage beast. Then deal with your situation as a cool and calculated reasoner.

The illusion that your livelihood is at stake is always an illusion.

The grocery-cart fear, the threatening idea that your pushing a grocery cart will follow a foreclosure notice as inexorably as the "camel's nose" or "mouse's cookie" story, is only a fear, a poltergeist with extreme unlikelihood and zero basis in reality.

A foreclosure proceeding is merely a request in court for rights to property to which you are legally entitled. Such an outrageous request requires an excessively high burden of proof. The nine tenths of the law pertaining to possession can all be marshaled in your favor. For the lender, one mistake invalidates the whole process: this is not true for you, who do not have the burden of proof and merely need to pick holes in the lender's burden. One sign of weakness can stall the process, if it can divert the lender into a different process. Judges love to say "why don't you two work it out," especially if a short sale or deed in lieu gives a convenient scenario to use this line.

Alternatives to foreclosure

There are so many ways to delay a foreclosure that "foreclosure defense" has become a great legal specialty. While we still insist that every process has a do-it-yourself track, foreclosure defense would require a whole additional book, and so legal/paralegal assistance is especially helpful here. A roadmap of options includes the following.

- Divert the lender into one of the strategies already discussed. A foreclosure presupposes that modification and refinance have already been attempted, so it can be stalled if some years have passed since the last such change or a revisitation is otherwise indicated. If you have prepared a short sale package or deed-in-lieu application in advance as a protective measure, when your lender files for foreclosure with the courts, you can submit the package to delay the foreclosure. Take counsel to choose your best options, and review all the strategies in this book thoroughly.
- In particular, prepare to present the lender, or the court if necessary, with the evidence you've accumulated of the lender's predatory practices or abandonment of its best interests: this can make the difference for bringing the lender back into a short-sale track, for instance. "Predatory" practices include unprecedented fees, any lender data falsifications or violations that you are aware of (although you may need to position yourself as entrapped if you had prior knowledge), as well as truly ridiculous securitization claims or balloon payments. Make a record of all current attempts to use other strategies and of all negotiator admissions that suggest undue lender resistance to your good-faith efforts. Evidence of such predation is useful partly to influence the judge but more to bring the lender back to negotiations.
- When your foreclosure is on the court dockets, you can also file paperwork suggesting bankruptcy, or a similar option called strategic default; as discussed, be prepared to push this threat to the brink, and be prepared for the consequences if your best decision is to take it over the brink. Strategic default represents the risk that you might succeed in maintaining other assets or even credit while neglecting both your mortgage payments -and- the duty of continuous negotiation availability that nonpayment carries with it. This should not be ignored.

- Mortgage reinstatement is an option that assumes the mortgage's original or modified terms can be brought back. This can be effective if circumstances change and can be a resolution recommended by you or a professional specialist.
- A "friendly lien" is a lien that you or a close associate place against your own property. For instance, if a business has been operated from home or you have rented it out, the secondary party may file a nominal lien against the property for reimbursement of any reasonable historical expenses. Because a proprietary or other business is a separate entity, even a business you have started and operated all by yourself can qualify for a claim on your property. The lien must naturally relate to documentable interest held by the lienor in the property.

If there are no other liens, some jurisdictions place your own lien first in line for repayment in foreclosure. This not only gives you a chance at proceeds from a foreclosure sale, but also reminds mortgagors that you're serious and need to be negotiated with, not fought against. A foreclosure defender can guide you whether this option will work for you.

Produce the note!

But what if no lender exists? You know, we've been calling these people "lenders" and "noteholders" even though we know some of them -have never held your note and have no proof they ever gave you a loan that requires repayment-. If you haven't found out who truly holds your note, it's time to start now. Widespread bankster gaming and mismanagement has led to some mortgages being totally unenforceable due to that excellent resource, "bank error in your favor." There are some debt instruments that nobody can enforce because -nobody legally owns them-. When other stall tactics have failed and you have your day in court, -demand the note-.

"Demand the note" groups, local meetup groups, and organizations like 877-YOU-KEEP 877-YOU-KEEP and the Consumer Warning Network have sprung up since widespread mortgage fraud became common knowledge around 2009. Such groups of homeowners are all helping one another with the process. Its great appeal arises from the liberating realization that literally any red-blooded American can demand his or her own note.

Mismanagement and sometimes outright fraud are evidenced in court anytime a lender claims to have a paper trail but cannot prove it. Speculative "wrapped," "flipped," and "rebundled" mortgages continuing through at least 2007 or 2008 have fractionated many loans irrecoverably: according to the Fed, almost 90% of all subprime mortgages are securitized. Employee confessions of approving thousands of foreclosures under oath, but without any verification of backup documentation, have spurred this trend. Judges nationwide are prone to throw any plaintiff out of court who can't find that blue-ink mortgage after a 30-day notice. The right to foreclose is possessed only by the original holder of the original (unphotocopied, nonelectronic) debt instrument, and that right is absolutely destroyed upon a confession that said instrument is "lost" and your well-established right to the evidence of your debt is only a "technicality." (The only alternative is to meet all Uniform Commercial Code requirements for enforcement of nonoriginal notes, which actually requires a higher burden of proof than just locating the original mortgage paper.)

Incidentally, one occasion upon with negligent mismanagement occurs is while repackaging the note during a refinance or modification. While most such transactions are documented correctly, we do hope you've availed yourself of seeking such a modification, and of using the mod as one rationale for justifying your demand for production of the mortgage note. The original note should be notated with any modifications or assignments, not electronically documented.

If you end up arguing this in court yourself, the demand itself is easy. The bulletproof argument to remember is this: if the court should grant a foreclosure against you when the instrument is admittedly "lost" and possibly in anyone else's possession, not only will you have the judgment to pay, but you will also be hypothetically immediately liable for the full mortgage if ever -

anyone- else claims (with or without evidence) that the instrument has been "found" again. Double jeopardy. Case closed.

In particular, watch for a lender filing that attempts to "reestablish" a lost note. This will amount to a stipulation that the note is lost and a request that the court ignore this glaring defect. Such an admission is the exposed jugular and you should file a motion to compel production immediately. The motion to compel is also filed if you've asked the lender to produce and 30 days have gone by unanswered (remember postmarks). Motions are usually filed with the clerk of court (who almost always has a helpful, communicative staff) and copied to the plaintiff's attorney.

When in court, watch for a claim that the lender has always held the note: you really will get to shout "Objection!" and explain that the lender assumed facts not in evidence.

About half of the United States, including Texas and California, allow out-of-court foreclosure sales, but you have exactly the same right to demand the note even in the absence of a court. The demands are made in writing and the steps are a bit more circuitous, but it's easy to find a group in your state that has experience demanding notes in nonjudicial proceedings. Since there is no court proceeding, upon receiving a "notice of intent" to foreclose (or a "notice of sale" scheduling the auction itself), immediately -instigate your own lawsuit- on the grounds that you require the court's intervention to prove formally the lender's authority to foreclose (viz., the note). This puts you on the same track with a little more effort. Use a paralegal or "pro se" research to ensure the court's filing and service requirements are all met.

Finally, adding a quiet title action to the mix, while it can be more expensive due to filing fees, absolutely gets the lender's attention for negotiation and loan modification purposes. Quiet title is an action that asserts ownership of the title and leaves other parties scrambling in a 30-day window to show cause why your ownership should not be recognized. The county recorder's lack of notices, liens, or assignments constitutes prima facie evidence of the lender having a flawed title and would supplement the action. When a lender has given you the runaround about other strategies but pursues foreclosure, quiet title and the risk that -you- might obtain a judgment against -them- both bring the lender back from being uncommunicative.

After demanding the note

- A complete overturn of its suit leaves the lender without standing. It is eminently proper to offer to conclude a sale or transfer (insist on full deficiency waiver) to salve the lender's wounds. It is also eminently proper to refuse the lender on the grounds that the real noteholder may turn up.
- If the ruling is either favorable or ambiguous, you can initiate a quiet title action later to perfect your ownership of title to the property.
- But even if the judge rules against you on the demand or defers the question, all is not lost. The lender has had an embarrassingly recorded warning that its papers are not in order. You still have time to regroup the shaken lender back into your preferred solution, such as deed in lieu or short sale. Since you've just filed an objection for the purpose of later appeal, the lender would much rather meet you at the negotiation table than in circuit court where it needs to shell out for its dream team. (And you don't need to be able to afford your own counsel: the threat that you might carry the day all by yourself later is sufficient to move the lender now.)
- Also, even if the judge allows a copy of the note, contrary to contract law, guess what: it's called "reversible error." Be on the alert for the possibility of such a flawed ruling and immediately object for the record, on the transcript or by a written motion, that such a ruling exposes you to double liability. While this objection may well be ignored by the trial judge, it will -not- be ignored by an appellate court, or by an appellate attorney you present the case to after it closes against you. This kind of double jeopardy can and does happen and is completely serious: one Tennessee homeowner was foreclosed against and evicted by Ameriquest in 2007 with zero note production, and she was shortly contacted by a completely different bank that claimed ownership of, and

demanded payment of, -the same note-. The perpetual credit risk she suffered should be proactively prevented by every judge who is warned about its potential for recurrence.
- In the less likely case that the lender produces a valid note, the matter is not over and you may still whip out an alternate "iron in the fire" that still salvages your preferences. One such productive response is a replevin motion, discussed in the next chapter. Production of the note does give the lender "standing" to continue in court, but that continuance may well result in pressure on the lender to successfully negotiate one of the delay strategies: you never truly know what they might admit in court that they really want.
- If the judgment is finally entered against you and remains unappealed, it's true that you generally face a bankruptcy blot and a seven-year bar to any but the most profligate credit. However, one option is to tie the matter up in appeals court if you have a compliant attorney, paralegal, or other representative. Another option is to sweat out the possibility that the lender will not enforce the eviction or judgment due to bureaucratic indifference. If your personal property is prepared for the possibility of a quick move (sheriff's evictions usually give you at least a few hours to organize your departure with remaining dignity), you might find that the eviction never comes. If your assets are protected and difficult for a collector to reach even with a judgment, the two-year statute of limitations might run out, after which a deficiency judgment will be unenforceable. Finally, in the worst case, the great American "safety net" of charitable institutions can always be approached for temporary shelter: after asking a court for mercy via bankruptcy, it should be easier to obtain mercy from a church.

In all our experience we have never personally known this worst case to arise solely out of a mortgage proceeding. The beast is toothless.

The fast track

Even though you're under the ultimate pressure, "demanding the note" and other foreclosure defenses can often deliver an outright win rapidly.

- Both a quiet title and a demand for production can be filed with the court independently. If the lender has not yet stated its "notice of intent" to foreclose, you can make an initial demand for production by writing the lender directly to accumulate an evidentiary response.
- If you are able to argue your case well in court, or you know someone who is able to, then you can proceed with carrying your demand for a note proving your (alleged) indebtedness before the judge, even in the worst case after foreclosure proceedings have already been initiated. If you are under the barrel, it may be time to make the attempt.
- If you can afford the action, a quiet title filing gives all interested parties 30 days to document their interest. This might clear your title, or its value might instead lie in forcing the lender to reveal its documentation. If the documents produced to claim an interest appear to be a flimsy excuse for an original note, this strengthens your demand for production in the separate foreclosure action.
- Any time the lender shows a sign of weakness, use the occasion to direct the process back into a less adversarial alternative strategy.

The delay track

You can still hold the moral high ground by demanding your rights and reparations to the very end, and deal out a surprise finish.

- Connect with a local meetup that assists people with demanding that their noteholders prove the indebtedness of the adverse possessor. Keep in contact over the months as foreclosure proceeds.
- A number of surprise filings and foreclosure defenses have been developed, including accusations of predatory practice,

threats of bankruptcy, demands for mortgage reinstatement, or friendly liens. In some cases these delay the process, in others they derail it cold.
- If the lender does produce the original note, thank them for their good recordkeeping and for defeating the claims of rivals and alleged assignees, and get to work renegotiating with them on a new footing.
- Don't forget your rights of objection and appeal, your rights of adverse possession, and your rights of asset protection, even in the case of rulings with which you disagree.
- "Loss" in court isn't the end of the world; it's merely the end of a misplaced hope. A positive attitude finds a way to work with even the most disagreeable demands.

Chapter 10

How We Left Debtors' Prison for Good

Let me share a few stories about how people managed the process of reclaiming their homes and escaping a debt of prison.

There's the inspiring story of the homeowners who "foreclosed" on the bank who had mishandled their mortgage and refused to do anything to correct it. The homeowners succeeded in getting deputies to threaten to lock the bank and impound the teller drawers before a bank officer arrived and met all their demands immediately. These homeowners got everything they asked for with a little creative negotiation.

The news reports teem with stories of successful demands for production:

- "A Pinellas County, Florida, judge denied Wachovia the right to proceed with its foreclosure against borrower Jacqueline O'Brien." (During continuance, Jacqueline obtained Wachovia's offer to renegotiate the loan, the ultimate goal she intended.)
- "In October 2007, Ohio Federal Court Judge Christopher Boyko dismissed 14 foreclosure cases brought by investors, ruling they failed to prove they owned the properties they were trying to seize."
- "In the loan business, the term [damaged goods] denotes ... mortgages where lenders misplaced crucial documents or applied rules too loosely" (a common occurrence as reported by Bloomberg).
- "The judge refused to allow a foreclosing mortgage lender to evict a homeowner facing foreclosure because the party bringing the foreclosure (HomEq Servicing Corporation) failed to prove (by presenting the necessary loan documents) that it was the correct party to bring and conduct the foreclosure proceedings" (U.S. Bankruptcy Court, Massachusetts).

- "The lender failed to either present the properly indorsed promissory note or any properly executed documentation establishing the chain of title supporting the lender's claim that it was the rightful owner of the mortgage. Accordingly, the judge refused to allow the foreclosure action to continue" (New York City trial court).

The following stories are other very illustrative examples of the never-say-die approach to asserting rights.

Suzanne sticks it out
While Suzanne's story is still incomplete, her transformation in taking on responsibility is quite instructive and hopeful for the future. Suzanne entered into a condominium agreement for a primary home on the advice of a Realtor relative, and eventually faced the same market downturn we all have. Her family's first attempt was to arrange a reverse mortgage for her because of advanced age. While this succeeded in providing temporary additional income, her equity was used up within years, her association fees skyrocketed in the meantime, and she was soon underwater not only in her home but also in her monthly budget.

Her second attempt, adopted in 2010, was in fact to "DO NOTHING." It's true that family difficulties, medical costs, and a dwindling retirement plan made decisionmaking that much more difficult. She began nonpayment not only on the mortgage but also on the association fees, on the argument that the association had failed to perform necessary remediation work for basic livability. This plan was able to squeeze her by on a tight monthly budget for two years.

Suddenly the association itself began demands for nearly $10,000 in fees owed in early 2012. This letter shook Suzanne into a serious reconsideration of options. Her third attempt was to obtain renters in the spare room of the condo that constituted her primary home. This succeeded in some months but not others. She then entered into a more mature and sincere fourth attempt that will reclaim her home more permanently. While her final decision has not yet been made, she has been hard at work (1) researching the original noteholder and the reverse mortgage holder to document irregularities in the mortgage and adverse lapses in the association's interests, (2) preparing her foreclosure defenses during the delay track, and (3) looking among her social circle for a white knight who can complete a short sale. Suzanne's attitude change alone is evidence that she will complete a successful negotiation to her distinct benefit.

MJ gets inspired

MJ and her husband live in Colorado in a primary home now valued at $330,000. They ran a small business and were able to keep current with a friendly lender until she and her husband began to lack satisfactory work in 2008.

- **First attempt:** Refinance. New terms were renegotiated successfully by Envision Lending. This allowed them to continue current payments for a year while searching for, but not finding, significant additional work. However, they became increasingly stretched by using up savings and rainy-day funds. Then the small lender went belly-up in 2009. When Bank of America stepped out of the woodwork claiming to be the new loan servicer, MJ was doubtful.
- **Second attempt:** Nonpayment. MJ began to invoke the right of collecting squatter rent (over $2,000 a month) rather than diverting it to the bank for a rapidly deflating property. Bank of America never received a nickel. At the same time, MJ obtained an equity loan and depleted her retirement and kids' college funds just paying current expenses for the next two years. Bank of America was essentially silent about the nonpayment and this encouraged MJ to continue, to the tune of over $50,000 of arrears.
- **Third attempt:** Negotiating during foreclosure. When Bank of America started pummeling MJ with foreclosure documents, she got serious. She had been waiting and hoping, relatively passively, that "something will turn up," while the family had been reduced to zero equity and to selling personal goods. It's true, answers do turn up, but the kind of answers that most people want turn up most often to those who do the most work. MJ used the occasion to start researching and handling communications with a property

manager for Bank of America that offered to help. She also obtained good advice from her support network and from a foreclosure defense specialist. In particular, she began a "produce the note" strategy. It turned out that she succeeded in verifying, in a single hour in the records of the county courthouse, that neither the original lender nor Bank of America had filed any records of liens, assignments, or other transactions with the county, under any variation of any party's name. This gave her high hopes that demanding the note and following up with quiet title would close the case.

- **Fourth attempt:** Friendly lien. MJ didn't rest on her laurels. Continuing to prepare for the case, she suddenly got inspired by the brilliancy of a friendly lien, an idea that meshed well even though she was completely out of petty cash. She remembered the successful but dormant small business she had run from her own home, and how she had an open offer, a few months prior, to revive it. She took the opportunity and made plans to become the first to file a lien against her own property to protect her business interest in it. Via existing family commitments, it was a small matter to ask for operating funding to reopen the shingle. Though it had other business opportunities, her company's first order of business of course was to file the lien against the property it used, namely, her house.

We have not yet heard the rest of this story, but MJ has now returned to her high hopes of getting by a few more years to retirement. By positioning herself to take advantage of two prongs at once (the lender's lack of documentation, and her own business's right to protect its interests by better documentation) she has a good strategy and a likelihood of victorious resolution. She is more excited than she has been for three years and it's clear the prisoner mentality has left the building.

Hannah closes the sale

Sometime after the mortgage bubble burst, one of our friends, Hannah, found herself juggling two investment condominiums alongside her primary house in South Florida. She had previously raided the primary equity of about $200,000 to speculate in the condos, a risk that went sour. One condo was in use, and the family member occupying the other had just died.

After taking some time to regroup, Hannah's first step was to look hard at her situation and take serious stock. She was underwater in all three properties and remained at risk of her investment continuing to lose value. While she was tempted to retain the investment in the hopes of rebound in the very long term, which is not unwise when one has the cashflow to hold out, Hannah came to admit that it's better to sell on the way down than to hit bottom without a cushion. Further, homeowner's association fees had nearly doubled because Hannah's neighbors were defaulting on what they owed the association. (Note that the right of nonpayment does not automatically extend to an HOA, because your maintenance fees are provided for services and upkeep rendered and are a contractual obligation that the HOA can enforce independently by a rapid court judgment: bailing out of this contract is not easily defended, nor easily converted into an adverse possession where it would stand on better ground.) Hannah ran the numbers and concluded that her overextension could not continue under any budget. She began attempting a permanent solution.

- **First attempt:** Hannah sought a refinance on the vacant condo. She was informed that the appraisal value had gone down so dramatically that it could not go through to her benefit.
- **Second attempt:** Hannah sought renters for the vacant condo. While this had sporadic success, its primary upshot was to demonstrate that reasonable rental payments, as determined by comparables, were -less- than the mortgage payments she was already indentured to pay! (The "Greater Fool" economic theory is that an investment is always valuable as long as you can find someone else to sell it to at the same price you paid. By definition, the hypothetical

buyer would be stupider than you because they are making the same deal as you did, only later. The harder such a hypothetical buyer is to find, the more you are likely to admit sheepishly that you were the most foolish party in the transaction.) While rental does provide temporary relief, exploring the option only served to confirm to Hannah that her original investment was mistaken.

- **Third attempt:** These fast-track options had one significant benefit to Hannah: they gave her time to commit herself to the long haul of short-selling one condo or both. She took another hard look, became an autodidact (a self-educated person), and considered and rejected the options of offering a deed in lieu and of doing nothing until foreclosed upon (these suited neither her situation nor her temperament). She then dove into a do-it-yourself short sale on the "delay track." While she initially attempted to keep all payments current, she soon recognized the liberating news that the short sale process would work better if she stopped paying on the vacant condominium: in a perverse actuarial paradox, lenders give more approvals for restructuring if you are in three months' arrears than if you're current.
- **Fourth attempt:** After Hannah began compiling her short sale package and hardship letter, she also wisely researched a secondary possible delay track, viz., bankruptcy. Consulting with an attorney left her with mixed feelings about bankruptcy as a necessary evil. She looked for a second opinion, found a helpful paralegal listed under "attorney alternatives," and decided to take a wait-and-see approach. In the end she decided against bankruptcy and was rewarded with successfully completing a short sale, which caused much less damage to her credit history than a bankruptcy would have.

Hannah followed the steps in chapter 6 very closely to accomplish her sale. The logistical details of paperwork and calculations are easier for a task-oriented seller, while the details of advertising and obtaining a written offer from a buyer are easier for a people-oriented seller, so it helps to be well-rounded. Pursue your strengths and then use the goal to psychologically motivate yourself to tackle any weaknesses. Hannah accomplished this by dividing all her details into bitesize pieces that could be accomplished day by day with visible progress and interim rewards. She advertised online and by word of mouth, and by continuous followup she eventually obtained a written offer from the condo's developer, who was interested in investment units. After five months of waiting on and following up with the bank, the sale was approved and completed. The bank refused a full deficiency waiver, but Hannah accepted this outcome because her promissory note was under $100 per month, compared to the mortgage, association, insurance, and tax payments. She considered this a successful resolution of the hit that she took from the market downturn.

Hannah isn't through

Spurred on by this success, she resolved to audit herself twice a year to keep on track to her financial goals. After another year she did the math and concluded that the second condo, with a purchase price just under $300,000, was also still on the way down and needed to be sold.

- **First attempt:** Since refinance looked unpromising, Hannah resolved to stick with a winner and complete a short sale before the new year was over. She began advertising on Craig's List and FSBO (the for-sale-by-owner website), and with printed an emailed picture flyers. She posted new ads several times a week and kept an organized file of every nibble so that she could respond immediately and follow up. She insisted on receiving written offers, even if they were ridiculously low, and promptly got an offer for less than $60,000. Though she knew it was likely to be rejected, she placed the finishing touches on a short sale package that she had otherwise already prepared, and sent it in anyway. The bank turned her down after two months.
- **Second attempt:** With continuous advertising Hannah was ready to create a second short sale package with a different buyer who was willing to commit to $65,000: it was harder to find a buyer because the lender insisted on qualified cash sales only. The negotiator even verbally approved the

package, but then ominously went on a long vacation starting the next business day; the bank assigned a second negotiator instead, who overturned the verbal approval and started from scratch. Though this sale was also rejected, the negotiator succeeded in approving the condominium association for mortgage sales as well as cash sales, which greatly broadened her search base; and she was also given the bank's all-important target number: a bottom line of $90,000.

- **Third attempt:** Hannah immediately returned to searching the expanded market and also contacting all her "nibbles," people who had shown prior interest. Within a short period she had a serious Craig's List offer that met the bank's criteria. This time there was no delay and the sale closed successfully in right at 60 days. Remember that to the degree her deficiency was not waived, she was scheduled to pay back no-interest promissory notes; and to the degree that it was waived, she was scheduled to receive a tax form reporting the degree to which the waiver was regarded as income and tax liability. However, compared to the stress and pain of the unbudgetable years, she was happy to be back servicing only one mortgage. We haven't done the math, so it's possible that her initial investment decisions, followed by short sales, may have set her original mortgage debt (plus the equity loan) back several years to its original value owed or even further back to a higher value. This is technically a loss, but it's one that was acceptable for the value of Hannah's education, not to mention the value she provided to her family and her renters.

Hannah has been so encouraged that she is now something of an evangelist for short sales. She is now doing a full accounting of her finances every six months and is occupied with teaching others the very methods described in this book.

Producing the note

One of our contacts filed a lawsuit against Wells Fargo to produce the note, based on the good-faith claim that it was necessary to prove they were the interested party with the right to sell his house. After some initial demurrals and complaints about the expense to which Wells Fargo had already gone to prosecute its rights, the lawyer capitulated and Wells Fargo (a better documenter anyway by all accounts) actually -produced the note- to everyone's shock. The homeowner recognized the form indented with his own signature and ink. The lawyer claimed that they finally concluded production was necessary to get the case over with and that they had previously declined because they didn't want to set any precedents.

The judge dismissed the homeowner's complaint with prejudice.

However, the homeowner didn't back down from his initial position. He wanted proof that Wells Fargo was the person of interest and he got it. It wasn't a bluff.

He regarded this as a win for several reasons:

- The rightness and validity of his request and methods were vindicated in court, even in a nonjudicial foreclosure;
- He obtained proof of the legitimacy of the Wells Fargo claim;
- He obtained proof of the illegitimacy of other claims (i.e., alleged assignments), a significant evidentiary gain;
- He obtained closure on how to proceed with the property;
- His faith in Wells Fargo was also rebuilt;
- His faith in the courts to protect homeowners against theft was restored;
- He was able to cede the property to Wells Fargo to sell for proceeds in good conscience, and turn to his two other houses.

While nonproduction victories are more dramatic, we wanted to illustrate a production victory as well, because the mindset and approach of this contact are spot-on. This story is not about winning a six-figure windfall on a point that the loser considers to be a technicality, but about escaping a Kafkaesque prison and trial and conducting a good-faith exit strategy with a partner that has proven trustworthiness in court.

The property was scheduled for sale and, upon closure, the homeowner has prepared a responsive replevin action. Because the sale closes out the mortgage, a replevin (a remedy to recover forms of withheld property) can then be filed to obtain back the original physical promissory note from the banker to the former homeowner. The great virtue in this is permanent insurance against the alleged assignee bank (which claimed to have received the note from Wells Fargo) ever coming back with an undead specter. This homeowner took charge of his destiny and escaped the mortgage for good.

Chapter 11

Take Courage and Stand Strong

You hold the keys to your own house. Nobody else does. We mean that in a metaphorical sense to convey several points:

- You hold the key to release yourself from prison. This key is the positive attitude that seeks and attracts answers to its questions and needs, with which you can move forward and continue the research necessary until you are certain of your own goals and the next step to achieving them.
- You hold the key to lock up the true prisoner of regulations, the lender. This key is your power to uphold the law and compel the lender to fulfill all its obligations, and your right to enforce those obligations, such as by nonpayment and adverse possession. You are free to display this key proudly on a chain like a warden, instead of throwing it out the window like a misanthrope.
- You hold the key to protect and shelter yourself. Because your possession has so many legal protections and there is such an industry committed to assisting you in enforcing these protections, your home can be your castle once again.
- You also hold the key to walk out with dignity anytime. While difficult mortgages are sometimes best resolved by yielding up a property to the demands of others, your right to have sufficient transition to find your next and better castle is also always upheld.
- You even hold the keys to your finances. These three keys are the power to budget, the power to negotiate, and the power to network. When in doubt, one or more of these three keys will work in any monetary lock: the resource can always be found somewhere among yourself, the other party, and a new third party.

While everyone else in the equation is churning through dozens of real estate cases to make a living, you and your friends and family are the only ones into your home in earnest. You're going to live there indefinitely; they're not. We call it a prison when it's not you but someone else freely using the keys to the building you live in. Why would you let anyone else claim any right to the keys to your castle?

In this edition of "Homestead Security" we've revealed several new strategies and the state of the art in liberating people from the tentacles of mortgages. We hope it's been a godsend to you. We're glad you've found the time and the place to sit down and read this far, and we trust that you have newfound strength to hold out for your rights to continue to have such a place as long as you continue working to show yourself worthy of it. We wish you the best as you take courage and step up to your destiny in reclaiming your home.

William Orion and Jana J. Perlman work in real estate to provide a radically different approach to property sales and management that not only respects real estate convention but also cuts through the red tape thoughtlessly wrapped around property owners.

www.ingramcontent.com/pod-product-compliance
Lightning Source LLC
Chambersburg PA
CBHW061515180526
45171CB00001B/182